HELP IN HARDSHIP

JAMES SZYMANSKI

ISBN 979-8-9915178-0-5

Book Cover by: Jason M. Bove with a contribution from Jessica Adenuga

CONTENTS

*In memory of Bonnie Mae Szymanski
and those who endure hardship*

ACKNOWLEDGMENTS

I began to write this book more than a decade ago when my daughter went through cancer treatment. Painful memories made it difficult for me to form my thoughts after her death.

I relate to a remark Charles Dickens made in his book *A Christmas Carol*. Ebenezer Scrooge asked the Spirit of Christmas Present about the fate of Bob Cratchit's son, Tiny Tim.

The Spirit envisioned Bob Cratchit's impaired movements after his child's death. I have found this true for myself after the loss of my daughter. My ability to move easily as I did in the past has decreased. I have slowed down significantly.

Since Bonnie's death, hundreds of people encouraged me to complete this book. Their prayers and support were a big reason I persevered through my distractions and struggles.

My coworkers also lovingly upheld me 'by prayer.' I will never forget their ongoing support through my long journey to get this book completed.

Many years have passed since Bonnie went through her cancer treatments. Yet I clearly remember the compassionate care given by medical doctors, physician assistants, nurses, and therapists.

Many non-medical people—hospital administrators, secretaries, patient transportation workers, cleaning people, and even parking lot attendants—blessed us with their compassionate words and actions. Their kindness, love, and concern are sweet memories I treasure today.

More than a dozen editors assisted me in the development of this book. To each one of you, thank you very much!

I am especially grateful for the assistance Larry J. Leech II provided me. As my writing coach he gave me valuable insights. The original study went from black and white facts to a technicolor account of impactful impressions made upon me through my hardships.

Special thanks to Crossway. Their permission to quote the ESV Bible verses referenced is appreciated.

Last, I want to thank the two most important people in my life—my wife Karen, and my Savior Jesus Christ. Karen supported and motivated me to get Help in Hardship completed. Jesus Christ provided enlightenment and direction as I developed this book.

Jesus Christ has renewed and transformed me. He gives hope to those who suffer, and a new life to those who trust in Him. To God be the glory!

INTRODUCTION

My wife Karen and I wanted children as newlyweds. For ten years we tried to conceive, and then God blessed us with our only child, Bonnie Mae.

I nicknamed my daughter Pumpkin. As an October baby, her bright, cheerful character gave me great joy as her father.

I enjoyed watching my daughter grow up and mature into an energetic youth. The many hours we played together in our free time helped us to develop a close relationship.

Bonnie and I were two peas in a pod. We thought alike and easily understood one another.

She had peace, love, joy, and firm faith in Jesus Christ. Bonnie also helped Karen and I understand each other better. Our daughter helped to produce a harmonious home environment.

The tranquility disappeared when Bonnie got diagnosed with cancer at 22 years of age. Most patients lived five years, or longer, after their therapy. Nonetheless, Bonnie died 12 months later.

When Bonnie died, I lost confidence, energy, and a clear

purpose in my life. I quickly understood how my only child had a profound impact upon me.

This book reflects my struggle through Bonnie's cancer journey, how God supported me after her death, and the importance of those who cared for us.

I first wrote *Help in Hardship* as a Bible study. This helped me to recognize God's undeserved kindness through my hardship. Then several years later, this book became my memoir.

This book is divided into three sections. The first five chapters look at my intense emotions. The next four chapters look at spiritual insights I gained during my hardship and loss. Those remind me of the unseen spiritual realm often unrecognized in the whirlwind of trial and loss. The final five chapters are topics I found helpful in my journey to restoration.

A decade has passed since Bonnie's death. I continue to gain valuable and needed insight from the Holy Bible. As I apply God's promises to my daily concerns, He reveals to me His matchless love and grace.

My personal experiences reveal how I moved from despair to hope and renewal. Each chapter concludes with Bible verses from God's Word. I do this because His Word is powerful and penetrates deep into the darkest soul.

I intentionally do not give names of individuals or places. Security, privacy, and conflict of interest are common concerns for writers. The few personal names mentioned are included with their permission.

My desire as you read *Help in Hardship* is to discover how trials develop a deeper relationship with Jesus Christ. He daily gets me through disappointment and painful struggles. I hope this book will also encourage you to trust Him every day.

CHAPTER 1
SHOCK

"While people are saying, 'There is peace and security,' then sudden destruction will come upon them as labor pains come upon a pregnant woman, and they will not escape."
1 Thessalonians 5:3

Despite the cold outside my home one February afternoon in upstate New York, I enjoyed my home filled with warmth, not just from the heat of a furnace, but from God's daily provision and protection. The future appeared bright, but an unknown event happened to change my life one afternoon.

My wife, Karen, and I were together at the kitchen table when we received an unexpected phone call from our daughter. At the time, she attended university and focused on her studies while on campus. She spoke to us every day after the completion of her classes. So, with a surprised voice my wife said, "Hi, Bonnie! What's up?"

She replied, "I'm in the library studying. I know there should only be one row of bookshelves where I am looking, but now I see two shelves." Bonnie went on to say she felt fine but requested for her eyesight to be checked.

Karen replied, "I'll call right away and make an appointment for you." I had no great concern for Bonnie, as she had an optometrist who took very good care of her eye problems.

This occurred in Bonnie's last semester of college. She intended to complete all her requirements in the three months before graduation, but circumstances quickly changed.

Bonnie's dilemma resembled my experiences with tornados in South Dakota. First there is a strange calm, and little time to prepare for what is to come. When the dark storm cloud hits the ground there is massive damage. My family experienced a similar situation and outcome.

INSTANT RESPONSES

When Karen called the optometrist's office, Bonnie's normal doctor was not available. However, another eye doctor looked at her the next day. The doctor gave no diagnosis for Bonnie's double vision. He just suggested she see an ophthalmologist for a more detailed exam.

Upon our arrival at home, Karen called a city hospital to make an ophthalmologist appointment. We were surprised Bonnie received an appointment for the next day. Normally it takes weeks, or months to see such a specialist.

The good news filled me with joy. I thought, "Wow, we were fortunate to get another doctor appointment so quickly!"

I did not notice any concerns about Bonnie's health. She experienced no major headaches, loss of energy, lack of sleep or change of appetite—all common side effects associated with a major problem.

At the hospital Karen went into the ophthalmologist

appointment with Bonnie. I thought Bonnie's examination would be done quickly, so I sat in the waiting area.

Her appointment took more than three hours. Even though Bonnie received immediate attention I reasoned to myself, "They probably overbooked and are behind schedule."

I had no reason to be alarmed or worried about Bonnie. Delays happen. I just needed to be patient. Plenty of interesting magazines helped me pass the time and kept my mind occupied.

IN THE DARKNESS

I rejoiced to see Bonnie and Karen after the appointment. The exam scheduled at 2:00 p.m. lasted for three hours, and then Bonnie needed an MRI. Thankfully it took only a few moments for Bonnie's scan to get done. As with the optometrist the day before, the ophthalmologist did not give us any information.

Daylight quickly turned into night. As I watched the February outdoor conditions change, I thought, "I need to get my family home soon."

We had an hour and a half drive through rural areas. So, as I drove home, my desire not to hit a deer on the dark slippery roads kept me on high alert.

Everyone was tired and quiet. I did not turn on the radio. Silence filled the car.

The quietness allowed me to think about my brief conversation with Bonnie's ophthalmologist. He referred to my daughter as an "interesting case."

His observation came as no surprise to me. I grew up with three brothers and no sisters. So I also found her very unusual. Men and women indeed approach life differently.

After decades of marriage, I continue to learn the ways of

my wife. As a father, I needed to discover how to raise a daughter.

Fortunately, Bonnie patiently endured my mistakes and made fatherhood easy for me. Most of our days concluded on a positive note in my effort to meet her needs as a father.

No one said what Bonnie needed to do. We all were concerned about the situation, but also had God's peace. We were confident her double vision problem would get cleared up. Then the seriousness of Bonnie's situation became known by an unexpected message.

FROZEN INSIDE

A warm house welcomed us from the frozen temperatures outside. Yet suddenly I noticed the blinking red light about a missed telephone call. The message made an uncomfortable chill go up my spine.

Bonnie's ophthalmologist requested us to call him back. Initially, I thought the conscientious doctor called to inform us what she had to do next.

However, the need to return the doctor's call immediately, without delay, raised a red flag within me. I came to a full stop, like one does at a red light. I paused a moment to pray, then called the doctor.

He informed me Bonnie's double vision occurred because of a tumor against her cranial nerve. I thought, "Uh oh, this is not good." Then my optimistic perspective kicked in. The doctor's voice sounded calm. He hoped the tumor would be benign. His response encouraged me to think, "Okay, it sounds like this is a fixable matter. She had battled through her previous medical setbacks."

The doctor suggested Bonnie see a neurologist. I did not like the idea of another doctor appointment. Bonnie carried a heavy workload at school. Academic demands required her full attention, not continuous visits to the doctor.

The thought of another long drive in winter weather, and the probability of another unconfirmed diagnosis caused me to have a delayed response. When I thought how the doctor went out of his way to see Bonnie, and even called us, I wanted to have the same concern for my daughter's health and restoration.

He made Bonnie's appointment with a neurologist at his hospital. The visit occurred a few days later, which gave me time to catch my breath. Her third doctor visit within a week made my head spin.

AN ANSWER

Bonnie's first two doctor visits occurred in the late afternoon. I attended her next appointment early in the morning to learn how the tumor and double vision would be treated.

As I joined Bonnie and Karen in the exam room, the doctor explained a little more about her brain tumor. However, he did not know how to proceed and referred us to a neurologist who does brain surgery.

Now we were to see the fourth different doctor in less than two weeks.

Bonnie's condition appeared to be very uncommon. No opinions or facts could be given about her situation, but I had an inner peace. God knew about her dilemma. So, I remained confident she would be okay. My hope of a miracle remained steadfast.

A few days later we met with an exceptional brain surgeon. He offered to do a biopsy. The procedure required an overnight hospital stay.

I use the word exceptional for a reason. The tumor resided

in an area of the brain which also controlled her heart and lungs. Any disturbance in the area could cause serious consequences. To get a biopsy of the tumor required great courage, confidence, and skill. Nevertheless, a small sample from the tumor gave needed insight into Bonnie's physical condition.

A few days later, the pathology report came through. Bonnie had a cancerous tumor.

SHOCKED

The news caused an uneasiness in me. Yet I trusted God to help us. He gives strength and hope to those who trust Him.

The diagnosis stunned me. The seriousness of her condition caused me to get disoriented. Daily choices such as what to eat or wear became a chore. I struggled with my confusion. Thankfully, my perspective changed as I refocused on Bonnie's concerns.

Her heart's desire was to graduate with her classmates. So, I informed her teachers about the need to finish her courses by correspondence. A few at first were reluctant, but then everyone agreed to help.

Not many cancer centers offered the type of treatment Bonnie needed. Karen and I struggled to find the right place for Bonnie's therapy. We wanted our daughter to focus on her studies so she could graduate.

As her parents we researched cancer centers where she could receive her treatments. We were discouraged, and weary. Nevertheless, we trusted God. He unexpectedly provided a place to stay while Bonnie received cancer treatment far from home.

THE EYE PROBLEM

Bonnie struggled with her double vision. She could not read easily. Prior to her tumor, Bonnie read several books for fun each month as she kept up with her schoolwork. The tumor hindered her vision, but she remained diligent in her studies.

Bonnie's optometrist recommended she wear an eye patch over her affected eye. In my sixty years of life, I knew of only two people who wore eye patches. One is a fictitious character, Nick Fury, in the Marvel Cinematic Universe. Moshe Dayan, an Israeli army commander, also wore an eye patch.

I make this point to show how unusual it is for me to see someone with an eye patch, which becomes the way I remember a person. It becomes part of their identity.

The only eye patch we could find was black. The patch stuck out from her eye, and Bonnie's glasses did not fit over it. We did not want Bonnie to be known for her black eyepatch. As her parents we raised Bonnie to be known for her character, not by what she wore.

Karen made several eye patches from soft, pretty fabrics. These allowed Bonnie to wear her glasses with the eye patch on. This reduced the focus on the eye patch in public. Later her optometrist put an opaque patch over one lens in her glasses. This helped Bonnie to read more comfortably with her glasses on.

ADDITIONAL ISSUES

An eye patch helped my daughter to read, but it also caused her to lose depth perception. Vision with one eye made Bonnie lose balance. Some days she returned home with bleeding hands and knees because of a fall.

The medicine to reduce inflammation of her tumor also

made it difficult for Bonnie to sleep. Her chemo doctor recommended she take the medicine in the morning, but the sleepless nights continued.

We were constantly tired. None of us did our activities with great anticipation or excitement.

Isaiah 40:30 reminded us how youths get faint, tired, and fall exhausted. Nevertheless, God raises up the weak and enables them to rise above hardship in His strength.

The shock and many side effects of Bonnie's chemo made it difficult for me to navigate my life. Yet God provided inner strength and supernatural endurance to get through the unexpected storm.

But I still experienced a heavy weight on my chest while I tried to support my family. I found it difficult to take a deep breath because of the burdensome pressure on me.

Several weeks passed before I could comprehend the immense challenge we were in. My perspective got clouded when I became exhausted and uncertain about the future.

NEEDED ASSISTANCE

News spread quickly about Bonnie's cancer. After we got the news, five neighbor ladies came at different times to pray with Karen. Each one came on her own to express their sorrow and prayed for my family.

We received hope in our trial as hundreds of people assured us of their prayers. Prayer involves a trust in God who lifts me above my hardship. Time and again the affliction departed from me when I knew about the support of others.

Often, I could only pray one word to God, "HELP!" My words and groans were inexpressible, but God knows my need even before I ask Him for His help.

I am grateful how He takes my sorrows and hardships upon

Himself. His powerful presence allowed me to know Him better through the trauma and confusion.

HELPFUL PROMISES TO REMEMBER WHEN IN SHOCK

"And he said, 'My presence will go with you, and I will give you rest'" Exodus 33:14.

"And Asa cried to the Lord his God, 'O Lord, there is none like you to help, between the mighty and the weak. Help us, O LORD our God, for we rely on you'" 2 Chronicles 14:11.

"Turn to me and be gracious to me, I am lonely and afflicted. The troubles of my heart are enlarged: bring me out of my distress" Psalm 25:16-17.

"My flesh and my heart may fail, but God is the strength of my heart and my portion forever" Psalm 73:26.

"Blessed is the man who trusts in the LORD, whose trust is the LORD. He is like a tree planted by water, that sends out its roots by the stream, and does not fear when heat comes, for its leaves remain green, and is not anxious in the year of drought, for it does not cease to bear fruit" Jeremiah 17:7-8.

"Likewise the Spirit helps us in our weakness. For we do not know what to pray for as we ought, but the Spirit himself intercedes for us with groanings too deep for words" Romans 8:26.

"But he said to me, 'My grace is sufficient for you, for my power is made perfect in weakness.' Therefore I will boast all the more gladly of my weaknesses, so that the power of Christ may rest upon me" 2 Corinthians 12:9.

"Therefore lift your drooping hands and strengthen your weak knees, and make straight paths for your feet, so that what is lame may not be put out of joint but rather be healed" Hebrews 12:12-13.

CHAPTER 2
NUMBNESS

"O death, where is your victory? O death, where is your sting?"
1 Corinthians 15:55

Numbness may not be the best word for how God comforted my wife and I after Bonnie died. We still experienced sorrow, grief and sadness. Nonetheless, our anguish and distress did not overwhelm us.

Bonnie's death did not have victory over our faith in Jesus Christ. Nor did the painful separation crush us. Why? My only explanation is His love and kindness, which go far beyond my own understanding.

The Bible does not use the word numbness. A similar expression used in Scripture is the word "kept." Kept can mean to be guarded, protected, or preserved.

God has always kept my family in His care. Over the past forty years, Karen and I have served Jesus Christ, and we have seen Him do great things.

I relate to what King David said in Psalm 68:19-20,

"Blessed be the Lord, who daily bears us up; God is our salvation. Our God is a God of salvation, and to God, the Lord,
belong deliverances from death."

The last three decades we have worked alongside the
African people. We have been blessed by their inspiring lives.

Most people we serve in Africa have few earthly possessions. Their difficult living conditions make everyday tasks a
wearisome challenge. They face life and death circumstances
on a daily basis. Many I assist have a deep faith. Their reliance
upon God motivates me to live likewise.

Karen and I continue to assist the people of Africa while
we live stateside. God uses our lives to inform churches in
America of practical ways they can assist Africans with their
spiritual, physical, and emotional needs.

The most difficult transitions in my life occurred when I
left Africa and after Bonnie died. Each time God helped me to
endure the painful separation.

LIFE IN THE FAST LANE

As a child, Bonnie accompanied Karen and I when we traveled
around America. We needed to visit the people who supported
us with their finances and prayers.

Along the way we often stopped to enjoy beautiful places.
We explored the Black Hills of South Dakota where we
watched prairie animals in their natural environment. We
picked up seashells on Florida's Sanibel Island. We also
marveled at the landscapes of Yosemite and Yellowstone
National Parks.

My family also enjoyed visits to Williamsburg and Mystic
Seaport. Those "living museums" helped Bonnie appreciate
history. At college she received a minor in history, then studied
in a graduate program to learn to be a librarian.

I always enjoyed our journeys. To see new places and meet old friends has always been a joy for me. On the other hand, Bonnie experienced America as a frantic blur from the back seat of the car.

She related our travels to a children's movie called *Turbo*. The story is about a snail. Snails are not known for their speed, but this slug received power and was able to race in the Indianapolis 500.

Bonnie did not like the long distances, nor the high speeds we traveled, to get across the country. Yet because of my work, she needed to go along with me and Karen. Our six-month furloughs required us to travel for medical checkups, to purchase supplies, as well as visit family and friends.

The trips were not enjoyable for Bonnie. She lived in constant instability and change. The need for Bonnie to be homeschooled while we traveled kept her occupied on our trips.

By the end of each furlough, Bonnie could not wait to return home to Africa. For two and a half years my daughter could stay in one place. There were no long, fast trips. She could also sleep in her own bed every night.

Life in the fast lane stopped. We enjoyed our African friends and the slower culture. Even our hardships became opportunities to grow closer as a family, and with God.

LIGHT IN THE DARKNESS

In Africa, water shortages, electrical blackouts, fuel rations, communication breakdowns, sickness and death were a daily challenge. We needed to plan ahead and be prepared for the shortages of water and electricity. These concerns required God's grace to supply the necessary provision for my family, as well as our neighbors.

A common sign painted on many cargo trucks said: "The only thing certain is uncertainty." No one knows the future or what will happen. In our city of at least a quarter million people, Karen and I did not expect such an unpredictable lifestyle when we first arrived.

We were in total darkness when the city power was out at night. We missed the hum of our fluorescent security lights outside. Darkness got so black I could not see my hand when pressed against my nose.

We were always aware how an unexpected attack could happen at night. People do evil things in the darkness so they will not be seen. Evil motivates people to do what is wrong before God and others. Such individuals are spiritually blind and hate the light of Jesus.

John 3:20-21 says, "For everyone who does wicked things hates the light and does not come to the light, lest his works should be exposed. But whoever does what is true comes to the light, so that it may be clearly seen that his works have been carried out in God."

We thanked God for His protection each morning when daylight arrived. Karen and I were relieved as many nights we had little sleep because of gunfire outside our home. We also thanked God that He kept watch over our daughter over those troublesome nights. Bonnie always had a good sleep. She rested in the fact Jesus kept her in His care.

NEED TO SAY GOODBYE

My family needed to endure frequent departures of good friends. Some were planned because of a change of location or a new job assignment. Other departures happened suddenly because of sickness or death. Expected or unexpected, the departures of our friends made me and my family sad.

Separations are difficult. Sometimes friendships are disconnected permanently. Nevertheless, I am comforted to know I may meet my friends again on earth. But if they love Jesus, I know I will meet them again in heaven.

The intensity of my goodbyes depended on the circumstances. Some friends came back after their furlough. Others never returned. I recognized life changes quickly, and is never the same again.

In times of sorrow, Jesus Christ comforts me as no one else can. The Holy Spirit keeps me close to Him. I am grateful to have experienced God's presence at the lowest times of my life.

SUPERNATURAL COMFORT

Hundreds of people prayed daily for Bonnie while she underwent cancer treatment. Several pastors also anointed Bonnie with oil as James 5:14 encourages for those who are sick.

Many times in Africa, my family witnessed God do miracles. We trusted Him to do a similar awesome work in Bonnie. Unfortunately, what I hoped for did not happen. My daughter's death hit me hard.

I responded to Bonnie's death with deep hurt. When I first learned about the cancer a year earlier, my reaction of surprise to her situation did not extinguish my hope for healing. Her death, on the other hand, devastated me. My permanent loss impacted me in a powerful way.

No medication or words of encouragement could cure my broken heart. Instead, God gave me something far greater—an inner calm. Jesus refers to this as peace. Karen and I appreciated help from outside sources, as well as the comfort offered by family and friends. But only God gives supernatural inner peace.

Jesus said in John 14:27, "Peace I leave with you; my peace

I give to you. Not as the world gives do I give to you. Let not your hearts be troubled, neither let them be afraid."

Bonnie's death upset me, but Jesus gave me relief. Like anti-itch cream on a mosquito bite, His consolation numbed the sting, and I received relief from my painful affliction.

Psalm 55:22 says, "Cast your burden on the LORD, and he will sustain you; he will never permit the righteous to be moved." God enabled me to be steadfast through this terrible time.

I trusted God to heal Bonnie, but she died. Thankfully, her death is not the end of her life. Her soul is now in heaven.

Nonetheless, I needed God's help to relieve my intense internal pain. The numbness He gave provided needed hope. God graciously comforted and strengthened me to endure my trial.

When I pray the Lord's prayer, I acknowledge His Lord-ship in heaven and earth. The heavenly home He prepared for me is yet to come. In the meantime, He provides for my needs and enables me to be right with Him. The unexpected peace and numbness He gave showed His love for me.

From my human perspective, the loss of my only child is hard to understand. As a father, I wanted to protect my daughter from her ruthless cancer, but all efforts failed.

The unanswered question of why my only child died at such a young age remains a mystery. I may never know why she died when she did, but that's okay. An answer would not change the outcome.

Now my desire is to learn more about God's love for me. As Isaiah 51:12 says, "I, I am he who comforts you." God's compassion has enabled me to experience His love. This encourages me to reassure others to trust Him when they go through hardships.

THE UNFINISHED LESSON

I originally wrote each chapter of this book while Bonnie went through her cancer treatments. I wanted to express my raw, painful experiences in an honest and truthful way.

The last chapter on peace was written in the hospital during the last few days of Bonnie's life. As her father, my heart broke to see Bonnie's health and life disappear before my eyes. Sadly, my prayer for healing did not happen as I expected. I felt hopeless.

Nevertheless, numbness and the Holy Spirit kept me focused on God. As Isaiah 26:3 says, "You keep him in perfect peace whose mind is stayed on you, because he trusts in you."

Bonnie's final days on earth were not a time when I would have expected to write about peace. Yet in my effort to learn how God gives help in hardship, I wrote down what He revealed to me. I continue to apply His Word to my life. Even after Bonnie's death, God continues to give me His peace as I trust Him.

This chapter on numbness is the only one I wrote after her death. I did this because I learned a very important lesson. Even in death, Christ's presence gives me unexpected comfort, and strength through my loss.

I daily think about my daughter. I am mindful how her death continues to impact me. I am grateful for God's restoration in my soul. Yet I know there are more lessons to be learned.

WHEN EXPECTATIONS ARE ABANDONED

Bonnie died in a hospital despite her desire to go home. Unaware Bonnie's death was so close, necessary preparations were made for her to return home.

A skilled craftsman from our church constructed a wheel-chair ramp to our back porch. When it was finished, the ramp reminded me of the wooden boardwalk at the bottom of Niagara Falls, well-built and strong.

Some neighbors turned our dining room into a bedroom space. A friend made new curtains to hang in the doorways between the dining room and kitchen, as well as between the dining room and living room. Another family helped remove the dining room furniture to make space for a hospital bed.

While these preparations were made at home, Karen and I stayed with Bonnie in the hospital. We were trained to use a Hoyer Lift to move Bonnie. We never anticipated doing such a difficult task. Nonetheless, Bonnie was paralyzed so we would need a lift to care for her at home.

Bonnie needed twenty-four-hour care. In the hospital many nurses and aides took good care of her. We were so grateful for their help.

God kept Karen and I from having to take care of Bonnie full time at home. We were prepared for what needed to be done, but thankfully God received our daughter into heaven from the hospital.

As Romans 9:15-16 says, "For he says to Moses, 'I will have mercy on whom I have mercy, and I will have compassion on whom I have compassion.' So then it depends not on human will or exertion, but on God, who has mercy." God is sovereign, compassionate, and merciful. Though my expectations were abandoned, God was gracious to help me.

UNABLE TO HEAR

A few weeks before Bonnie's life ended, she received additional radiation. This photon radiation caused damage to her vocal cords.

Because of the damage, she could not speak loud enough for me to hear what she said. My constant requests for her to repeat her words made Bonnie frustrated and sad. The hospital offered the use of a microphone, earphone, and an amplifier, but I still struggled to understand her. Bonnie got so weak she could not communicate clearly. Thankfully, the nurses who helped my daughter had better comprehension of her concerns.

My inability to communicate made me wonder what God wanted me to do. I was confused yet God carried me through this difficult time.

Psalm 27:5 reminded me, "For he will hide me in his shelter in the day of trouble; he will conceal me under the cover of his tent; he will lift me high upon a rock." I repeated to myself He will, He will, He will keep me.

I knew my own weakness as my mind and spirit were overwhelmed. With the help of God's Spirit, I responded with confidence when important decisions had to be made.

A CHALLENGING WEEK

God helped me successfully accomplish difficult tasks immediately after Bonnie's death. The responsibility to choose a casket, secure a burial plot, order a headstone, and obtain funds to cover the costs were all unexpected, but necessary tasks.

I also wrote a brief reflection about Bonnie's life for the funeral bulletin. Then I needed to choose songs for her funeral.

Bonnie's viewing and funeral service took place one week after her death. Hundreds of people came to these public events. Friends waited in long lines to express their sorrow to Karen and me.

At Bonnie's viewing, Karen and I stood for more than five hours near her open casket. At the bottom of her casket lay a crocheted Captain America shield a friend had made for Bonnie.

Karen and I were not near one another at Bonnie's viewing. As a slow processor, I often depend on my wife to help me remember names. To my surprise, I recalled everyone's name as the long line of people expressed their sorrow, many I had not seen in years. With each visit I also realized how God empowered me to stand for hours in my weakness.

I often looked at Bonnie's lifeless body next to me. The experience seemed like an unwanted dream. To speak of her in the past tense reminds me that she is no longer with us. Yet the touch of each person gave me empowerment, and much-needed comfort while I grieved.

The next day friends and family gathered for Bonnie's funeral service. Many people publicly spoke about how Bonnie's life had influenced them. Their kind words blessed me.

I appreciated the testimonies of how my daughter impacted so many people. Their reflections reminded me how nothing on earth, no spiritual power, nor even death keeps us from God's love. He gave everyone who spoke the ability to rejoice, not only for Bonnie's life, but also praised God for His goodness.

Bonnie's cancer journey gave me a new perspective on life. Even though her departure is still emotionally hard on me, God lifts me above my grief.

He comforts me through my difficult times. He helps me in unexpected and amazing ways. I know He is near. God is my strength as He numbs the painful sting of loss and helps me in my weakened condition.

HELPFUL PROMISES AND ENCOURAGEMENT WHEN IN NEED OF GOD'S NUMBNESS

"The eternal God is your dwelling place, and underneath are the everlasting arms" Deuteronomy 33:27.

"The Lord is the strength of his people; he is the saving refuge of his anointed. Oh, save your people and bless your heritage! Be their shepherd and carry them forever" Psalm 28:8-9.

"For thus says the One who is high and lifted up, who inhabits eternity, whose name is Holy: 'I dwell in the high and holy place, and also with him who is of a contrite and lowly spirit, to revive the spirit of the lowly, and to revive the heart of the contrite'" Isaiah 57:15.

"Even to your old age I am he, and to gray hairs I will carry you. I have made, and I will bear; I will carry and will save" Isaiah 46:4.

"For I know the plans I have for you, declares the LORD, plans for welfare and not for evil, to give you a future and a hope. Then you will call upon me and come and pray to me, and I will hear you. You will seek me and find me, when you seek me with all your heart" Jeremiah 29:11-13.

"Blessed be the God and Father of our Lord Jesus Christ, the Father of mercies and God of all comfort, who comforts us in all our affliction, so that we may be able to comfort those who are in any affliction, with the comfort with which we ourselves are comforted by God" 2 Corinthians 1:3-4.

"Humble yourselves before the Lord, and he will exalt you" James 4:10.

"Humble yourselves, therefore, under the mighty hand of God so that at the proper time he may exalt you, casting all your anxieties on him, because he cares for you" 1 Peter 5:6-7.

CHAPTER 3
ANGER

"Be angry and do not sin; do not let the sun go down on your anger."
Ephesians 4:26

From a very early age, Bonnie always enjoyed a good story. As a child, Karen and I read her children's books before she went to sleep. Bonnie could listen to the same story over and over.

Sometimes, in an effort to know if she was still awake, I would insert a different word into the story. Without fail Bonnie replied, "Oh Daddy, it doesn't say that!" Bonnie developed good reading and comprehension skills.

Bonnie loved to study the Bible. She also enjoyed "The Chronicles of Narnia" series written by C.S. Lewis. There are a lot of biblical references in the series, but they are not directly identified as such. Yet Bonnie understood the dynamics of each character and location Lewis wrote about.

Bonnie enjoyed reading about a person who changed their behavior. She watched for what motivated them to become a likable character.

MY FAVORITE MOVIES

When Bonnie and I watched movies together, she often explained to me how and why the character change happened. We both found humor and joy watching the process of how an unsettled soul becomes content.

The "Cars" movie series by Pixar personally hit home for me. Each movie has a message I identify with from my life. The first movie looks at adjustments needed when life in the fast lane slows down in a rural community. The second movie reveals how misguided opinions arise when one is not aware of cultural practices. The last movie looks at how outside influences affect those who do not desire or expect change.

Lightning McQueen is the main character in each movie. He is a red race car who hates to lose. McQueen is self-centered, arrogant, prideful, insensitive, judgmental, and driven to win. Early in the story, Lightning has no idea how his actions impact others. Then unexpected events make a significant alteration in his behavior and relationships.

I appreciate the humor and creativity given to each motor vehicle in the series. Each has a unique personality. The color, size, function, age, and condition of each vehicle gives an image of how they are viewed by others.

Lightning McQueen reflects the character of people who have not been transformed by Jesus Christ. Ephesians 2:1-5 describes how everyone has rebelled against God. No one is born "good," or naturally lives in obedience to God. I thank God for how Jesus transformed my life from bad to good.

The "Cars" movies reveal how anger causes irrational behavior and dead-end results. Anger is used as motivation for needed change. This is why Ephesians 4:26-28 says I can be angry, but not respond with evil intentions.

When I get angry, I am thankful how Christ motivates me to do what is right instead of what is wrong.

A NECESSARY CHANGE

While I wrote this book, my old car needed major repairs. Instead of paying for repairs I decided to buy a new car. Change is always part of life. Yet I am grateful how God's Word NEVER changes. He is always dependable, and faithful to get me through unexpected circumstances.

My new car gets me from place to place but has caused a significant change in how I drive. The car is equipped with several safety features, including an automatic slowdown feature. This causes my car to slow down when it senses another vehicle in front of me.

I have driven cars and trucks for many decades. I know how to manage an automobile. The safety override is what I normally do myself. My inner Lightning McQueen comes out when this happens. I get upset when I cannot make my own decisions. I have never driven a car like this before, but it is the trend in new cars.

I am not comfortable with how my car makes decisions for me. The slowdown feature frequently takes me by surprise on the highway, especially when I need to pass others safely. My momentum to pass another vehicle is lost when the car suddenly slows down by itself.

This new feature also gives me a false sense of security. The automatic slowdown stops me, but I must never get lazy when I drive. I always need to keep full attention on what is ahead of me and behind me.

When this feature prematurely slows down my car, it delays my response to maneuver through heavy traffic. I get distracted by this safety feature. So now I pass slower vehicles quicker before more traffic arrives behind me. This allows me to make safer lane changes and have a clear view of potential obstacles.

I have read the owner's manual to understand my new car better. Familiarity with the new features allows me to be in better control of my vehicle. I drive with a greater awareness of potential concerns.

I now respond in an appropriate way to my car. Rather than get frustrated with it, I identify what triggers me to get angry. I anticipate the car's response for a more pleasurable ride.

The Holy Bible is my dependable manual to guide me through life, especially in regard to my anger.

THE ONE TRUE OWNER'S MANUAL

Throughout Bonnie's cancer treatments, and after her life ended, I received comfort from God's Word. Psalm 119:105 describes His Word as, "a lamp to my feet, and a light to my path."

The Holy Bible helps me respond in appropriate ways when I get angry, irritated, or confused.

The Scripture reminds me to be aware of my ungodly emotions. Great changes happen within me when I seek the help of the Holy Spirit, instead of relying on myself.

Hebrews 4:12 says, "For the word of God is living and active, sharper than any two-edged sword, piercing to the division of soul and of spirit, of joints and of marrow, and discerning the thoughts and intentions of the heart."

His Word has gone deep into my heart. Since God came into my life, I am aware of behaviors I need to change. The Bible teaches me God has a purpose for my life. His Word motivates my heart to seek Him as He guides me through life.

MY HEART AND GOD'S HEART

People today are encouraged to "follow their heart." However, the Bible teaches me to obey God.

Deuteronomy 11:16 says, "Take care lest your heart be deceived." Jeremiah 17:9-10 also warns, "The heart is deceitful above all things, and desperately sick; who can understand it? 'I the LORD search the heart and test the mind, to give every man according to his ways, according to the fruit of his deeds.'"

God knows what is on my heart and mind. When I trust Him, He enables me to make changes in my life. After my daughter died, my anger caused me to recognize I had a problem. I had to admit I had a problem with anger in order to deal with it.

James 1:19 reminds me to think before I speak. What is on my heart does not always reflect the thoughts God has about me. The words I speak have the power to encourage, or discourage, myself as well as others.

My negative self-talk isolates me from others. A statement such as 'I am not able to do anything right,' creates a counter-productive thought in me. I may think my situation is hopeless, but God does not want me to think in such a way.

My anger became a motivation for me to seek God's help. I daily want Him to develop in me a deeper love for Him, myself, and others. God gave me the answer to my dilemma.

MY NEED TO OBEY GOD

I do not understand God's purpose regarding the loss of my daughter. Yet her death motivates me to seek Him.

God is good and great, but He did not give me the miracle I desired. This caused me to get angry at God and others. I became self-focused, and unable to respond with kindness.

Jesus warns us in Matthew 7:1-3, "Judge not, that you be not judged. For with the judgment you pronounce you will be judged, and with the measure you use it will be measured to you. Why do you see the speck that is in your brother's eye, but do not notice the log that is in your own eye?"

When my relationship with God got disconnected, I lacked the ability to recognize or discern God's will. I was unable to identify deceptive messages designed to misguide me.

Genesis 3:1 shows how Satan caused Eve to doubt God. Satan asked, "Did God actually say, 'You shall not eat of any tree in the garden?'" No, God did not say those words! Genesis 2:16-17 says, "And the LORD God commanded the man, saying, 'You may surely eat of every tree of the garden, but of the tree of the knowledge of good and evil you shall not eat, for in the day that you eat of it you shall surely die.'"

Every tree in the garden provided good fruit to eat. Only one tree produced a fruit that would cause death. Satan knew this fruit would reverse the direction of God's perfect plan. Adam and Eve were deceived to disobey God.

Like Adam and Eve, I am also tempted to respond in ways God does not intend for me. My refusal to obey God causes a separation between me and Him. James 4:17 says, "So whoever knows the right thing to do and fails to do it, for him it is sin." I need God's help to be in right relationship with Him.

I need to discern God's truth from what is a lie. My choice determines if I intentionally obey Him or live a life of self-righteousness and sin. When I neglect God's Word, I cannot recognize my self-centeredness.

What used to be clear and undeniable suddenly gets confusing. My anger grew as I blamed others and condemned myself. This behavior led me into a downward cycle of self-defeat and placed me in a deep pit where I felt abandoned by God.

NO SLOWDOWN FEATURE

Earlier I explained how the slowdown feature on my car makes me angry. It takes away my ability to handle my vehicle as I see fit in order to proceed. The only option I have with a slowdown feature is to reduce my speed before it stops me.

This makes me angry because I like to reach my destination in the fastest time. Yet sometimes conditions require me to slow down.

Unlike the "safety" innovation in my car, I have no override to control me. As a believer in Jesus Christ, I am aware of my sinful nature within me.

Thankfully, the Holy Spirit gives me the ability to respond appropriately when I have a problem. Anger is like a warning light on my dashboard. It informs me of a problem before a major breakdown happens.

I am aware how I can deny my problem and believe detrimental thoughts instead of trusting God's Word. There is also the temptation to satisfy my sinful nature with drugs, alcohol, or an ungodly lifestyle. Yet I know problems only multiply when I rebel against God's desire for me.

When I depend on myself, unexpected circumstances often cause me to get angry at God. When I get stressed, I become angry easily and little things annoy me. My sinful nature is always with me. I can stop God's Spirit from working in me. First Thessalonians 5:19 warns, "Do not quench the Spirit."

God does not automatically slow me down or keep me from get getting angry. I need to be aware of my emotions. When I am able to identify the source of my anger, I can ask God to help me keep my emotions under control.

Otherwise, I get antagonistic which causes me to isolate myself from others. When my relationship with God is out of tune, I make the effort to reconnect with Him.

As God helps me in my hardships, He gives me hope. He enables me to see beyond my hopeless condition. This is why I daily ask God to take control of my life. He helps me to intentionally pursue Him by faith. This requires confidence in His ability to provide what I need to get through my hardship.

HELP FROM THE HOLY SPIRIT

The valiant efforts of many to eradicate my daughter's cancer failed. The outcome has been difficult to comprehend. But through all the uncertainties and hardships, God gave me the ability to persevere through my painful loss.

First John 3:24 says, "Whoever keeps his commandments abides in God, and God in him. And by this we know that he abides in us, by the Spirit whom he has given us." I am grateful how the Holy Spirit reminds me of God's Word and helps me to know Him better.

Bonnie's cancer caused me great sorrow and disappointment. Nonetheless, God's Spirit has comforted me in my despair and anger. I recognize my need for God to help me in my struggle.

I needed to humble myself before God in my weakness and put my trust in Him. James 4:6 says, "God opposes the proud, but gives grace to the humble."

My loss gives me an increased awareness of those who go through hardship. I am much more sympathetic to those who hurt than I was in the past.

The Holy Spirit has transformed me through difficult

times. I realized my need to trust God in a greater way. John 12:24 says, "Truly, truly, I you say to you, unless a grain of wheat falls into the earth and dies, it remains alone; but if it dies, it bears much fruit." Submission to God has produced more Christlikeness within me.

As I trust God my faith grows, and He fills me with His peace. God restrains my anger as He gives me inner contentment. I take comfort in His Lordship over me as He transforms my life.

My human nature wants me to depend on my own self-reliance. Thankfully the Holy Spirit reminds me that God is in control. When I am stressed, I take a deep breath then release it slowly. My ability to let go of inner anxiety and anger helps me maintain a hopeful outlook.

First Corinthians 2:9-10 says, "But, as it is written, 'What no eye has seen, nor ear heard, nor the heart of man imagined, what God has prepared for those who love him'- these things God has revealed to us through the Spirit. For the Spirit searches everything, even the depths of God."

I know God is my Creator. He is good and never harms me. I trust Him to make all things right in His time. The Holy Spirit is faithful to remind me of my constant need for God. Still my anger and pride continue to challenge me. I rely on God to transform and restore me as I struggle.

The temptation to reject God's way is an ongoing battle within me. Do I trust my emotions, and depend on my own understanding? Or is my confidence in what God teaches me through His Word? Thankfully God's Spirit helps me to discern what I need to do to stay faithful to Him.

God's Spirit is gentle and gives me great comfort. The awareness of God's presence assures me of His desire to help the brokenhearted. Through my tragic experience, I have kept my hope in God. Romans 5:5 says, "And hope does not put us to shame, because God's love has been poured into our hearts through the Holy Spirit who has been given to us."

Negative thoughts and anger arise in me, but His Spirit calms my soul. Scripture reminds me of my need to trust God. His Word has changed my outlook through the help of the Holy Spirit. My hope in Christ allows me to anticipate a better day yet to come!

MOVED IN AN OPPOSITE DIRECTION

When Bonnie died, my emotions sank. My energy, optimism, and contentment disappeared.

I did not want to stay in this condition. My anger increased since I could not stop the inner pain on my own. My inadequate efforts gave me little relief. Thankfully, as I humbled myself before God, He changed my outlook.

Jesus Christ gave me hope and purpose. My slide into anger and despair was a natural response to loss and death. Nonetheless, the Holy Spirit comforted me so I could experience God's peace.

My frustration and anger tend to increase when I trust in my own understanding. However, when I apply God's Word to my life, I am transformed by the Holy Spirit.

In John 14:6 Jesus said, "I am the way, and the truth, and the life. No one comes to the Father except through me." Jesus is the only way to know God's truth and have eternal life. The only way I can find satisfaction and purpose in life is through Jesus Christ.

Jesus is my Lord and Savior who has given me the ability to respond in appropriate ways. As a follower of Jesus Christ, I have received the Holy Spirit. He empowers me to do what is right as God desires.

The "fruit" of the Holy Spirit mentioned in Galatians 5:22-

23 can be compared to a seed God has planted in me. The seed of God's Word produces what He desires as His Holy Spirit helps me to live for Him.

HELPFUL PROMISES AND ENCOURAGEMENT WHEN ANGRY

"It is the LORD who goes before you. He will be with you; he will not leave you or forsake you. Do not fear or be dismayed" Deuteronomy 31:8.

"The LORD passed before him and proclaimed, 'The LORD, the LORD, a God merciful and gracious, slow to anger, and abounding in steadfast love and faithfulness'" Exodus 34:6.

"But know that the LORD has set apart the godly for himself; the LORD hears when I call to him. Be angry, and do not sin; ponder in your own hearts on your beds, and be silent. Offer right sacrifices, and put your trust in the LORD" Psalm 4:3-5.

"A hot-tempered man stirs up strife, but he is who is slow to anger quiets contention" Proverbs 15:18.

"Return to the LORD your God, for he is gracious and merciful, slow to anger, and abounding in steadfast love" Joel 2:13.

"The LORD is slow to anger and great in power" Nahum 1:3.

"Let all bitterness and wrath and anger and clamor and slander be put away from you, along with all malice. Be kind to one another, tenderhearted, forgiving one another, as God in Christ forgave you" Ephesians 4: 31-32.

"Know this, my beloved brothers: let every person be quick to hear, slow to speak, slow to anger; for the anger of man does not produce the righteousness of God" James 1:19-20.

"No one born of God makes a practice of sinning, for God's seed abides in him, and he cannot keep on sinning because he has been born of God" 1 John 3:9.

CHAPTER 4

FRUSTRATION

"But now thus says the LORD, he who created you, O Jacob, he who formed you, O Israel: Fear not, for I have redeemed you; I have called you by name, you are mine."
Isaiah 43:1

When my wife and I learned about Bonnie's cancer, we were confused and frustrated. Nevertheless, we were united in the effort to fight Bonnie's cancer.

The frustration we experienced can be described by the old expression, "stuck between a rock and a hard place." None of us knew how long, or even if the therapy we chose would be successful. However, we were determined to proceed with hope.

Before Bonnie began treatment, we studied all the different treatment options for her particular type of brain cancer. Some procedures seemed to be better than others. We wanted Bonnie to have the best outcome.

The procedure we chose was proton radiation. This required Bonnie to get treatment at a cancer center located a two-day drive away from our home. We left our comfortable home and went to an unfamiliar place so Bonnie could receive treatment to suppress the growth of her tumor.

We did not know anyone who lived near the cancer center in Indiana. The doctors who treated our daughter were confident they could help her.

Our dear friends in New York prayed for us as we trusted God on this uncertain journey. Even though we would be far from one another, their support went with us in prayer. We were not alone as we faced unexpected circumstances.

After decades of service to Christ, Karen, Bonnie, and I enjoyed the assurance of God's faithfulness. When this difficult situation arose, our close relationship with God helped us through this hardship.

LONG TERM IMPACT OF FAITH

Faith involves trusting God to fulfill His promises. Faith also requires hope that what we do not see will happen.

Many people thought Bonnie's situation appeared hopeless. Yet God gave us strength and security in our weakness to persevere. My family expected God to heal Bonnie.

God encourages me to come before Him with my burdens. He knows my troublesome circumstances before I even speak to Him. When I talk to God about my problems He calms my anxious heart.

First Peter 5:10 says, "And after you have suffered a little while, the God of all grace, who has called you to his eternal glory in Christ, will himself restore, confirm, strengthen, and establish you." Jesus Christ makes me right with God. There is nothing I need to do before my Almighty Creator will accept me.

Religion gives people man-made rules they need to follow

before their god accepts them. However, the Holy Bible teaches that God wants His people to have a relationship with Him. He desires me to love Him as my Savior and obey His Word.

When I know what the Bible says, but fail to obey God's commands, I am at risk of a serious downfall. I must do what the Bible says. As Jesus said in Luke 6:46, "Why do you call me 'Lord, Lord,' and do not do what I tell you?"

As I learn to apply Scripture to my life, God's Spirit can work in me. The entire Bible is historically accurate and trustworthy. This is why I desire to learn from Him every day through His Word.

Many people think they are right with God but have no desire to follow His Word. Jesus will sadly tell them one day, "I never knew you" (Matthew 7:23) because they did not make Him Lord of their lives.

I am thankful Jesus redeemed me. Redemption means Christ paid the price for my sin when He died on the cross. But I had to accept His free gift of salvation personally.

Romans 6:23 says, "For the wages of sin is death, but the free gift of God is eternal life in Christ Jesus our Lord." My redemption in Christ is freely given but came at a great price. God's only Son, Jesus Christ, gave His life for me so I can have eternal life in Him.

Bonnie, Karen and I chose to live by faith in Jesus Christ. Through His trustworthy Word, we kept our eyes upon Him. Our faith in God is no temporary hope, but rather a daily trust in Him. He never forsakes those who love Him, no matter how hopeless life appears.

A TREACHEROUS JOURNEY

The hospital in New York that discovered Bonnie's cancer wanted to begin treatment immediately. We had one week to research other treatment options.

We spoke to a doctor in Indiana who thought he could help. He had experience with Bonnie's type of cancer. This gave me hope.

We were not sure if the Indiana cancer center would take Bonnie as a patient. She needed to be evaluated there first.

This required a quick trip to Indiana. On the journey we had an overnight stay in Cleveland, Ohio. Thankfully we had no bad weather along Lake Erie that day.

At daybreak we continued our journey westward. As soon as we drove into Indiana, a blizzard came upon us. The bad weather caused us to slow down to a snail's pace. Our day turned dark well before we reached the cancer center. I tried to go as fast as I could, but my stress level made me irritable.

I asked Karen and Bonnie to pray for me. They did so in a calm and quiet way. Their voices did not reflect my inner turmoil. They expressed their confidence in God, and in me to get through the storm. Their prayers provided the comfort and encouragement I needed.

We reached our destination much later than I expected, but we were all grateful for our safe arrival. I grew up in an area where winter storms were common and made travel dangerous. Terrible accidents happened in white-out conditions. I did not make the successful journey on my own. It was by God's grace.

We were grateful the Indiana proton cancer center accepted Bonnie as their patient. We immediately informed the New York hospital of our decision to get treatment at another location. Then we drove home to gather items for our temporary stay in the "Hoosier" state.

Thankfully, six weeks of proton radiation slowed the growth of Bonnie's brain tumor. When treatment was completed in Indiana, we returned to New York and settled back into our home.

THE UNEXPECTED HAPPENED

We were grateful Bonnie had few side effects from her radiation treatments. Bonnie felt good but got tired easily.

The doctor in New York who initially found Bonnie's cancer, kept a close watch on her tumor. Six months later, MRI images found Bonnie's tumor was growing. The tumor began to cause havoc in her body. Nearly one year after the discovery of Bonnie's cancer, Karen and I found ourselves uncertain about our daughter's fate.

Bonnie got admitted to the New York hospital for additional treatment. It was an extremely cold winter. The outdoor temperatures stayed below freezing for over a month. The dark cloudy days generated a lot of snow. Winter weather caused hazardous driving conditions, but I also recognized my own bleak outlook.

Before Bonnie received admission into the hospital, I obtained a handicapped parking permit. This helped her as I was able to park closer to building entrances. It also helped me. I was emotionally handicapped due to my daughter's declining health.

Throughout Bonnie's hardship my entire family continued to trust God to heal her. Then after she died, I got frustrated. I struggled with her death. My emotional distress troubled me, but I never lost faith in my Savior Jesus Christ.

Jesus once asked His disciples if they would always follow Him. Simon Peter responded with an inspired statement in

John 6:68 when he replied, "To whom shall we go? You have the words of eternal life."

Like Peter, I am convinced Jesus is the only way to eternal life. He has given me a new life in Him. I daily cling to Him, and trust Him to help me through each day, especially when I am frustrated and discouraged.

Many years have passed since my daughter's death, and I miss her every day. Yet I am grateful how God continues to carry me through my disappointments, weaknesses, and sorrows.

MY LIFE IN CHRIST

God can do the impossible, even when I am insecure, lonely, and annoyed. I am grateful for the Holy Spirit who helps to guide my thoughts and actions.

As I live under Christ's Lordship, He empowers and comforts me in extraordinary ways. In the dark, difficult, and disturbing times of life, Jesus keeps me strong when I recognize my own weakness.

First John 4:9 says, "In this the love of God was made manifest among us, that God sent his only Son into the world, so that we might live through him." Christ's forgiveness has given me a new outlook on life.

I am thankful the Holy Spirit motivates me to live for God. Christ's forgiveness has transformed my life through the Holy Spirit. He empowers me to overcome my weaknesses as the Holy Spirit lives within me.

Ephesians 2:4-5 says, "But God, being rich in mercy, because of the great love with which he loved us, even when we were dead in our trespasses, made us alive together with Christ-by grace you have been saved." Indeed, Jesus has saved me. I have purpose, hope, and peace in this turbulent world.

God gives me contentment when I am frustrated. He gives me patience and strength when I am weak. My challenges motivate me to learn more of Him as I experience His help in hardship.

A TIME TO GROW

I like to garden but will not plant seeds outdoors in the winter. Patience is needed until spring when the ground gets soft and warm. Seeds grow best when they are planted at the proper time and under the right conditions.

Renewal also happens at the appropriate time. Ecclesiastes 3:1 says, "For everything there is a season, and a time for every matter under heaven."

Karen and I have made significant adjustments together. Over the years we moved many times, experienced health issues, and lost our only child. Each transition required us to support and encourage each other. We lived by the truth of Psalm 46:1, "God is our refuge and strength, a very present help in trouble."

When Karen married me, she took on a new surname. Prior to our marriage she knew herself by her maiden name. Her new last name, Szymanski, is not an easy name to say. Most people make several attempts to verbalize my name before they pronounce it correctly.

Over time Karen not only got used to her new last name, but she also identified herself as my wife. Karen willingly accepted me as her husband. She is my companion who has made my life complete.

At our wedding ceremony, we sang a song to one another. Little did we know the importance of this song, especially after the death of our daughter Bonnie. The song, "In His Time" by Maranatha music, reflects our commitment to Christ.

This musical composition expresses our trust in God. As a married couple we believe God makes all things beautiful in His time. The marriage vows we made at our wedding ceremony became a lifelong commitment. We made a steadfast promise to accept, love, and honor one another as long as we live.

Frustration and disappointment have happened in our marriage, especially when my words are not said in a proper way. Afterwords, I have needed to acknowledge my self-centeredness and reconcile with Karen.

When we are both injured by what is said or done, restoration requires our desire to change. This happens along with God's help. We pray Psalm 51:12, "Restore to me the joy of your salvation, and uphold me with a willing spirit."

So, we daily humble ourselves before God and ask Him to work in our lives. He then empowers us to love each other and have unity in our marriage.

When we humble ourselves before God, our pride and selfishness diminish. A desire for harmony refreshes our relationship. Through genuine remorse, forgiveness, and encouragement we support one another to keep our bond strong.

A secure relationship, and thoughtful companionship, are foundational to our marriage. The Holy Spirit then enables us to live together in harmony as God desires.

Winter, spring, summer, and autumn have unique characteristics. Each season brings changes. Over the years, I have recognized the different seasons Karen and I have gone through in our marriage. Through those transitions we allowed Jesus to be our strength and guide.

As I live my life for Jesus, He helps me make needed adjustments in my behavior. As I respond to Karen with His love, we find ourselves content to be with one another. Whatever the problem, Jesus helps us get through the difficult transitions and helps us make needed changes.

PREPARATION FOR THE STORMS

The song "In His Time" begins with an acknowledgment of God. He is acknowledged as our unique Almighty God. The words: His, He, Lord, You, and Your are used throughout the song's introduction. He is a personal and relational God who cares for us.

Karen and I sang this song together as a prayer to God. We believe He is the Holy, perfect, Lord of His creation, as well as the ultimate source of authority and beauty.

"In His Time" concludes with a confession and a commitment to God. From our wedding day to the present, we daily dedicate our lives and marriage to Him. Each morning we read Scripture to one another, and pray together. This is done with the conviction God will show Himself to us and work in our lives as we trust Him.

To start my day in such a way helps me remember Karen's concerns. I also think about what I read in the Bible, and how He wants me to live for Him.

The interactive relationship I have with God helps me to have a close relationship with Him. I gain a greater awareness and appreciation for what He reveals around me. As God enlightens me to see things from His perspective, He prepares me to respond appropriately to the challenges I encounter.

My relationship with God helps me to be assured and confident in my life. I am more content and less troubled in frustrating situations. I have learned that in His time, God is able to restore what has gone wrong.

The transition or change I hope for may not always

happen, but I trust God. I have faith to believe He will provide what I, and others, need. I rest in His amazing grace.

At night, before Karen and I go to sleep, we again pray together. We give Him thanks for what we were able to do throughout our day and give Him our burdens so we can rest. The reminder of His ongoing presence gives me peace and comfort to have a good night's sleep.

I do not deny that I face many frustrations in life, but I leave my burdens with God. He is faithful to strengthen and restore me and helps me to persevere.

While in great pain and frustration Job expressed a similar trust in God. He said with assurance, "For I know that my Redeemer lives, and at the last he will stand upon the earth. And after my skin has been thus destroyed, yet in my flesh I shall see God" (Job 19:25-26).

Before Job died, he experienced God in powerful ways. I, too, have learned that I need to trust Him in my frustrating circumstances.

God is at work in me as I obey Him. He makes all things right in His time. As God's child, I receive His love and care when circumstances are out of my control.

ANXIETY AND FRUSTRATION

Isaiah 11:2 speaks of seven ways the Holy Spirit works in my life. "And the Spirit of the LORD shall rest upon him, the Spirit of wisdom and understanding, the Spirit of counsel and might, the Spirit of knowledge and the fear of the LORD." In other words, the Holy Spirit lives in me. He gives me rest, discernment, insight, guidance, strength, peace and a godly fear.

I have no need to be afraid of God. He desires me to acknowledge His authority in my life. When I do so, the Holy

Spirit makes Himself known to me. I expect God's Spirit to work in me, and daily welcome Him to help me through my hardships.

Most English translations of Psalm 23:6 say, God's goodness and mercy 'follow' me. The Hebrew word 'follow' can also mean to 'give pursuit.' God is always active, and aware of my situation. He encourages me to know Him better.

When I am frustrated, I wonder, "Why do I feel far from God?" He has not moved. I am the one who has drifted away from God. He knows my frustration. He knows everything about me. Psalm 139:2 says, "You know when I sit down and when I rise up; you discern my thoughts from afar."

When I am tempted to lean on my own understanding, the Holy Spirit reminds me to trust God. James 5:7 refers to the importance of perseverance. "Be patient, therefore, brothers, until the coming of the Lord. See how the farmer waits for the precious fruit of the earth, being patient about it, until it receives the early and the late rains."

Delays are opportunities for me to learn from God. I usually do not know why something is delayed in my life. Nonetheless, what Psalm 27:14 says is true. "Wait for the LORD; be strong and let your heart take courage; wait for the LORD!"

GOD KNOWS MY ANXIETY

When I began my career in Africa, my first employer asked me to resign after four years of working with them. Shortly thereafter, another group wanted me to work in their organization. However, I first needed to raise financial support to live overseas and provide for my family. Many people knew me, and my love for the African people. However, it took four years to raise the required financial support.

Throughout this time many people I respected encouraged me to change to a different type of work. In my heart, I knew God wanted me to persevere and return to the work I loved. So, while I waited, I asked God to reveal if my pride, or any other issue, was preventing me from returning to Africa.

God never directed me to change my pursuit. Instead, as I prayed, He kept me hopeful. I did not allow my anxiety or the delay to keep me from the work I desired to do.

Psalm 139:23-24 reflects my prayer when I am confused. "Search me, O God, and know my heart! Try me and know my thoughts! And see if there be any grievous way in me, and lead me in the way everlasting!"

God graciously allowed me and my family to return to Africa. I have worked three decades with the organization who encouraged me through my wilderness experience, and I continue to work with the African people.

More importantly, I learned through my delay. Hardship and frustration caused me to draw close to God and develop a closer relationship with Him during that difficult frustrating time.

I came to better understand why God kept my family in our unwanted situation during that time. Both of Karen's parents, and my father died while we waited for the needed financial provision to serve Him overseas. We were able to assist our parents when they needed support before they died. They also would not have known Bonnie if our effort to be in Africa sooner had not been delayed.

I learned to trust God and His faithfulness. He has kept me on His straight and narrow path. First Peter 2:21 reminds me to be faithful. "For to this you have been called, because Christ also suffered for you, leaving you an example, so that you might follow in his steps."

God created me and put me in a right relationship with

Him. Through His Son Jesus Christ He has made me His beloved child. The painful outcome of Bonnie's death still disappoints me. It is a reminder of the broken world I live in. Yet, "Even before a word is on my tongue, behold, O LORD, you know it altogether" (Psalm 139:4).

God was faithful to provide me what I needed as I trusted Him in that frustrating time. He still does! God declares in Isaiah 45:5-6, "I am the LORD, and there is no other, besides me there is no God; I equip you, though you do not know me, that people may know, from the rising of the sun and from the west, that there is none besides me; I am the LORD, and there is no other."

HELPFUL PROMISES AND ENCOURAGEMENT WHEN FRUSTRATED

"Where shall I go from your Spirit? Or where shall I flee from your presence? If I ascend to heaven, you are there! If I make my bed in Sheol, you are there! If I take the wings of the morning and dwell in the uttermost parts of the sea, even there your hand shall lead me, and your right hand shall hold me. If I say, 'Surely the darkness shall cover me, and the light about me be night,' even the darkness is not dark to you; the night is bright as the day, for darkness is as light with you" Psalm 139:7-11.

"He has made everything beautiful in its time. Also, he has put eternity into man's heart, yet so that he cannot find out what God has done from the beginning to the end" Ecclesiastes 3:11.

"Therefore do not be anxious about tomorrow, for tomorrow

will be anxious for itself. Sufficient for the day is its own trouble" Matthew 6:34.

"And when he got into the boat, his disciples followed him. And behold, there arose a great storm on the sea, so that the boat was being swamped by the waves; but he was asleep. And they went and woke him, saying, 'Save us Lord; we are perishing.' And he said to them, 'Why are you afraid, O you of little faith?' Then he rose and rebuked the winds and the sea, and there was a great calm. And the men marveled saying, 'What sort of man is this, that even the winds and sea obey him?'" Matthew 8:23-27.

"So Jesus said to the Jews who had believed him, 'If you abide in my word, you are truly my disciples, and you will know the truth, and the truth will set you free'" John 8:31-32.

"Therefore, as you received Christ Jesus the Lord, so walk in him, rooted and built up in him and established in the faith, just as you were taught, abounding in thanksgiving" Colossians 2:6-7.

"Watch yourselves, so that you may not lose what we have worked for, but may win a full reward. Everyone who goes on ahead and does not abide in the teaching of Christ, does not have God. Whoever abides in the teaching has both the Father and the Son" 2 John 8-9.

"You therefore, beloved, knowing this beforehand, take care that you are not carried away with the error of lawless people and lose your own stability. But grow in the grace and knowledge of our Lord and Savior Jesus Christ. To him be the glory both now and to the day of eternity. Amen" 2 Peter 3:17-18.

CHAPTER 5

DEPRESSION

"For the Scripture says, 'Everyone who believes in him will not be put to shame.' For there is no distinction between Jew and Greek; for the same Lord is Lord of all, bestowing his riches on all who call on him. For 'everyone who calls on the name of the Lord will be saved'"

Romans 10:11-13.

When my daughter died, my life descended into darkness. Life which once appeared bright and clear became much more complicated. My disturbed emotions and unsure thoughts caused me to be unsettled. Daily activities lost their purpose and the excitement they once provided.

Depression and frustration are closely related. When I am frustrated, I am still motivated to pursue my goals. On the other hand, when I am depressed and discouraged, I develop a critical outlook.

I lose my confidence and clear direction when frustration turns into depression. My optimistic outlook can easily get abandoned when discouragement overtakes me.

I struggled with depression after my daughter died. Yet the promise of Romans 10:13 is true. Jesus daily rescues me, especially in difficult days when He comforts me as I struggle with my depression.

Jesus constantly gets me out of my deep emotional pit as He places me upon a solid rock. I know the huge impact Bonnie's death has had on me, but I cannot change the outcome. Thankfully God has helped me to have a hopeful outlook about my purpose here on earth.

BLESSED BY JESUS CHRIST

I never 'got over' my daughter's death. Nevertheless, I have an eternal hope. The Bible teaches life on earth is temporal. Yet God's promise of an eternal home with Him gives me assurance of a better tomorrow.

While I await the glorious place God has prepared for me, He comforts my soul with inner contentment. Jesus said in John 16:20, "Truly, truly, I say to you, you will weep and lament, but the world will rejoice. You will be sorrowful, but your sorrow will turn into joy."

Life on earth is far from perfect, yet I enjoy God's presence with me right now. Even though life gets dark and sorrowful, the Holy Spirit changes my outlook and gives me a new direction.

Romans 5:2-5 says, "Through him we have also obtained access by faith into this grace in which we stand, and we rejoice in hope of the glory of God. Not only that, but we rejoice in our sufferings, knowing that suffering produces endurance, and endurance produces character, and character produces hope, and hope does not put us to shame, because God's love has been poured into our hearts through the Holy Spirit who has been given to us."

When depressed, Jesus unveils new insights to me through the Holy Spirit. He reassures me of God's intention to use my life here on earth. He knows my heart and my weaknesses. To Him my faith is far more valuable than fine gold. My intense and painful trials become a way I can honor Christ.

As 1 Peter 1:7 says, "so that the tested genuineness of your faith-more precious than gold that perishes though it is tested by fire-may be found to result in praise and glory and honor at the revelation of Jesus Christ." When dejected, discouraged, and disheartened, faith in Jesus Christ enables me to keep my hope in Him.

Restoration from depression is a process. As Christ restores my darkened soul, I recognize that supernatural change does not happen by my own efforts. The Holy Spirit inspires me to be hopeful about what I cannot see. He reminds me of God's promises that keep me confident in His dependable mercy.

When a person asks me, "How are you doing?" I frequently reply, "Blessed." Blessed is a descriptive word, meaning fortunate, contented, and grateful. This does not mean I have no troubles in life, but I am confident God is in control. He is with me in my hardships and gets me through them.

Blessed can also mean happy. The fact that I do not carry my burdens alone comforts me. God has reduced my stress. Christ calms my troubled soul through His assurance in the Bible of a better life to come.

He promised in John 11:25-26, "I am the resurrection and the life. Whoever believes in me, though he die, yet shall he live, and everyone who lives and believes in me shall never die. Do you believe this?"

I not only believe in Christ's resurrection over sin and death, but daily experience His renewal in me. As I give Him my stress, sorrows, burdens, and discouragement, He comforts me. His strength upholds me in my weakness.

To learn what God desires in my marriage, Karen and I daily read the Bible together, then we pray. Second Corinthians 1:9-10 reflects our condition, "Indeed, we felt that we had received the sentence of death. But that was to make us rely not on ourselves but on God who raises the dead. He delivered us from such a deadly peril, and he will deliver us. On him we have set our hope that he will deliver us again." God has been faithful to give us a strong relationship with Him and in our love for one another.

HOPE AND DEPRESSION

My solid foundation in Christ provides me a secure assurance of God's help in hardship. Depression is an ongoing battle, but my fears and depression are reduced by the help of the Holy Spirit. God gives me liberty from the inner slavery of despair and hopelessness.

Before I gave my life to Jesus Christ, sin kept me in bondage to my evil thoughts. My natural desire to do wrong could not be kept under control. My inexcusable behavior made me depressed. I knew my thoughts and actions were not right with God.

Now as I intentionally live by God's Word, my life is transformed. I know His power to save me and enlighten me in this spiritually darkened world. Christ's restorative work in me is not the result of my own efforts. Rather, as I trust Him, He empowers me to do His will in my life. I take no credit for what God does through me. Instead, I am humbled and grateful for His help every day.

The words "faith" and "hope" are not wishful thoughts. They are grounded in an expectation of a certain outcome.

Depression happens when loss occurs. The permanent separation from my daughter caused me to be depressed and confused. My irreplaceable loss caused a lack of sleep, rest, and appetite. My shortage of energy and strength left me irritated, discouraged, and without direction.

Job 4:25-26 describes my condition when I am depressed. "For the thing that I fear comes upon me, and what I dread befalls me. I am not at ease, nor am I quiet; I have no rest, but trouble comes."

Thankfully the Holy Spirit helps reduce my stress, sorrow, and confusion. When things do not work out as I expect, the Holy Spirit reminds me of my need to trust God to transform me.

I am grateful Isaiah 58:11 is true, "And the LORD will guide you continually and satisfy your desire in scorched places and make your bones strong; and you shall be like a watered garden, like a spring of water, whose waters do not fail." Through the Holy Spirit, God guides, satisfies, and strengthens me.

A LESSON FROM JONAH

When Jesus lived on earth, many people watched Him do great miracles. He knew their thoughts and said to them, "This generation is an evil generation. It seeks for a sign, but no sign will be given to it except the sign of Jonah" (Luke 11:29).

Jesus spoke of "the sign of Jonah," which refers to His death, burial, and resurrection. Like Jonah's three nights in a large fish, Jesus returned to life after His three-day confinement in the grave.

Jesus explained this to His disciples in Matthew 12:40, "For just as Jonah was three days and three nights in the belly of the great fish, so will the Son of Man be three days and three nights in the heart of the earth."

Jonah experienced a miraculous work of God at sea. He

survived three days in the stomach of a great fish. Jonah under-stood God punishes those who disobey His Word.

God wanted Jonah to tell the people of Nineveh of their need to repent and obey God. When he did so, they turned from their evil ways, and God spared their lives from destruction.

Like the people of Nineveh, I also need to obey God's Word. When I do so, He comforts me with His merciful grace.

Christ's resurrection from the dead, gives me an optimistic hope in His ability to transform me. Because Jesus is alive and reveals Himself to me, His Spirit motivates me to intentionally seek Him in my life.

Many times, I fail to recognize what God desires me to do. My lack of attention and self-focus keep me preoccupied with myself. I fail to respond as God desires.

The Holy Spirit reminds me how my short sightedness, and empty accomplishments never satisfy me. I am satisfied when I obey Jesus Christ. Even when I am frustrated and disap-pointed, Jesus is faithful to remove my burden when I ask for His help.

Many times, I become overwhelmed and depressed. Then I lose hope. This happens when my desires are not met. The sign of Jonah gives me hope when I am discouraged. I am able to face my pain, insecurity, and sorrow. The Holy Spirit comforts me when I am heartbroken.

Like Jonah, I struggle with despair. My troublesome thoughts cause me to doubt God. I get depressed and disori-ented when discouragement reinforces my hopeless condition.

As 2 Corinthians 3:14,16 say, "But their minds were hard-ened. For to this day, when they read the old covenant, that same veil remains unlifted, because only through Christ is it taken away." "But when one turns to the Lord the veil is removed."

When we invite Jesus into our life, he removes the veil and allows us to understand the Bible. When I humbled myself and asked Jesus into my heart, I turned away from spiritual darkness. The Holy Spirit then helped me to understand God's Word.

I am still aware of my need for Christ when inner conflict causes me to lose heart. When irritated, I trust the Holy Spirit to keep me calm through my struggle. He renews my hope when I am discouraged.

My anxieties and fears are reminders of my fallen human condition. Thankfully, Christ helps me to recognize I am unable to change my hopeless condition by myself. I am grateful Jesus has saved me from my self-destructive behavior. He empowers, guides, and shapes my character through the Holy Spirit who lives in me.

As Romans 8:6 says, "For to set the mind on the flesh is death, but to set the mind on the Spirit is life and peace." Indeed, life without Christ only leads to a painful death. Thank God He made a way to be right with Him through His Son Jesus Christ.

Fear, discontentment, and depression can be overcome with the help of the Holy Spirit. In John 14:16-18, Jesus refers to the Holy Spirit as our counselor and helper. Even though I struggle with depression, God's Spirit comforts me when I trust Him. I know He will never leave me nor forsake me.

WHEN TAKEN DOWN

I sigh a lot since my daughter died. I miss her and am thankful Jesus has calmed my wounded heart. I am aware of my need to consciously 'look up' when I am depressed and in need of God's comfort.

Like Jonah, I struggle with troublesome thoughts. When I

get overwhelmed and depressed, I often neglect God. My discouragement turns into hopelessness, and I lose heart.

As Psalm 38:8 says, "I am feeble and crushed; I groan because of the tumult of my heart." When my mind and emotions are disturbed, I can lose hope and fall into depression.

As a young boy, I would spend hours picking up flat stones to throw them across calm water in the creek near my house. When a stone jumped five or six times over the surface, I got excited. This motivated me to throw another stone and try to make it leap farther. With each attempt, the stone eventually dropped into the water.

As I have grown older, I have learned circumstances happen in a similar manner. I step out by faith into deep waters. Then when complications arise, I begin to sink like the stone because my momentum is lost.

When Bonnie went through her cancer treatments, I knew we were in deep waters. Everyone in my family had faith God would restore her life. But she died, and I sank into depression.

After her death I cried out to God in prayer, just as Jonah did in the belly of a large fish. I did not write down my prayer, but it was probably similar to Jonah's prayer, "I called out to the LORD, out of my distress, and he answered me; out of the belly of Sheol I cried, and you heard my voice. For you cast me into the deep, into the heart of the seas, and the flood surrounded me; all of your waves and your billows passed over me" (Jonah 2:2-3).

I relate to Jonah as he described his situation. While trapped in a giant fish he became surrounded by darkness. My circumstance also put me in a dark place where I did not want to be. I had no way to get out of my dilemma through my own efforts.

My emotional struggle gripped me with dissatisfaction and

sorrow. Many times, I felt like Jonah, a person who was thrown into stormy waters.

When I find myself dragged under by strong emotional currents, I want to reach solid ground, but destructive forces are at work to give me doubts, fears, and discouragement. These challenges motivate me to stay close to Christ.

GO AGAINST THE CURRENT

Strong water currents can pull a swimmer far out to sea. The natural response is to swim directly toward the shoreline, but the undercurrent is so strong a swimmer cannot swim straight to shore because of the undertow.

When a swimmer finds himself in such a situation, he needs to swim parallel to the shore in order to get out of the undercurrent. Eventually, there will be a calm place in the deep water where he can get safely back to solid ground.

Bonnie learned to swim when she was in first grade. A nearby school offered classes where Bonnie gained confidence in her swimming skills.

As mentioned earlier, I enjoy skipping stones over calm water. Bonnie on the other hand wanted to be in the water as much as possible. Rather than practice her swim strokes, she dove into the water like a dolphin.

Bonnie would come up briefly to the surface to catch her breath, and then immediately dive back down. Often Bonnie intentionally threw items into the pool so they would sink to the bottom. She then dove down to retrieve them.

She allowed the wind and waves to pass over her in deep water. Bonnie's confidence in uncertain situations kept her calm. Her strong relationship with Christ gave her assurance as she trusted Him.

Bonnie lived as a person who loved God. She stayed true to

God and obeyed His Word. Her faith in Christ shined for all to see.

As her earthly father, I daily committed my daughter to God. When we were apart from one another, I prayed for God's protection and guidance upon her.

My prayer reflected the desire described in Ephesians 1:16-19. "I do not cease to give thanks for you, remembering you in my prayers, that the God of our Lord Jesus Christ, the Father of glory, may give you the Spirit of wisdom and of revelation in the knowledge of him, having the eyes of your hearts enlightened, that you may know what is the hope to which he has called you, what are the riches of his glorious inheritance in the saints, and what is the immeasurable greatness of his power toward us who believe, according to the working of his great might."

To live an empowered life in Christ requires the help of the Holy Spirit. It also requires an intentional desire to go against the strong current of ungodly beliefs. I am grateful how God's Holy Spirit works in me, even when I am depressed. God daily enlightens my heart. He reminds me of His immeasurable greatness.

God wants me to trust Him when I am weak. As I believe in Him, I fight the urge to let fear overwhelm me. The Holy Bible describes this as spiritual warfare against the forces of darkness or evil.

Second Corinthians 10:3-4 says, "For though we walk in the flesh, we are not waging war according to the flesh. For the weapons of our warfare are not of the flesh but have divine power to destroy strongholds." This is why when I am depressed, I trust in God to change me by His mighty power.

A WONDERFUL LIFE

I am grateful to remember the many happy times Karen and I enjoyed with Bonnie. Those moments together did not only influence our daughter, but they also reminded us of our own childhood experiences.

The Christmas movie, *It's a Wonderful Life,* gives me memories of my youth. The classic black and white film causes me to think back to when life seemed innocent. Bedford Falls is a fictitious location, but the cities of Buffalo, Rochester, and Elmira mentioned in the movie are places I knew of as a child.

Few people know that Elmira is where Samuel L. Clemens, better known as Mark Twain, wrote his classics, *The Adventures of Tom Sawyer* and *Huckleberry Finn.* Those books, referred to in the movie, also influenced my desire to discover new and unknown places.

This motion picture takes place between the 1930s and 1940s. Those were the years of my parents' youth. They told me about similar experiences they had to those in the movie.

The main character, George Bailey, reminds me of how I also needed to navigate through unexpected and difficult hardships. Bailey had a business partner who unintentionally lost his money.

The financial crisis, along with his personal concerns, caused George to become deeply depressed. He attempts suicide but is rescued by an angel named Clarence.

The movie opens with George Bailey's friends praying for him. Their prayers are being heard in heaven. This awakened my own memory. In a similar manner, hundreds of people prayed for my family through Bonnie's cancer journey.

I am confident God responded to each of their prayers, just as He did for George Bailey. God provided many angels to help me through my hardships.

My experiences of unexpected and supportive encounters with strangers while Bonnie received treatments often happened in hospital hallways. When I left Bonnie's room after my overnight stay with her at the hospital, people recognized my distress. Many spoke words of encouragement, and some even stopped to pray for me while we were in the hallways of the medical center.

God supplied me with needed care in ways I never expected. Even the parking lot attendants showed their concern and support as they always asked about my daughter's condition.

The 1946 version of *It's a Wonderful Life* gives an excellent reminder of the environment my parents experienced. Today I live in a new millennium, where lifestyles are different, but where God still works in unexpected ways. I am grateful how He has given me a wonderful life here on earth.

I experience difficulties daily. Nevertheless, God helps me to be still, and to trust Him when life does not go well. When I rest in Him, He reveals Himself to me and gives me His peace.

LOOK UP!

After Bonnie died, I got into the habit of looking down at the ground. I took more notice of the dust on my shoes than anything else around me.

One afternoon as I walked alone on a lonely dirt road, God instructed me to "look up." I immediately responded to the request and lifted up my head. As a slow processor, I wondered what I needed to see or do.

But I obeyed the quiet and gentle voice of God as He spoke to me. I stopped to notice the leafless trees around me. The bark of each tree stood out while I observed their different textures, colors, and shapes.

My eyes gradually looked beyond the trees. I began to admire the warmth of the brilliant sunlight and appreciated the beautiful blue sky above me. My world of gray suddenly became colorful.

From that point on, sights, sounds, smells, taste, and feelings were reawakened in me. The veil of depression lifted. I began to appreciate life as God wants me to experience it. A transformation happened within me.

I no longer needed to focus on my dirty shoes. Rather I made an effort to look up and see beyond myself. There was a whole new world God wanted me to see and appreciate. I began to be aware of and thankful for His undeserved kindness in my depressed condition.

Every day I consciously look for new insights in my daily activities. Not everything I experience is pleasant and peaceful. However, the Holy Spirit who lives in me shows me how God's presence is with me.

I have hope of a better day to come. Most days are a challenge to get through, but God is gracious to comfort me. Life here on earth is far from perfect but I am daily reminded to trust Him. He is aware of my struggles and helps me through them.

When I get discouraged, I talk to God. I am confident He is with me and keeps me from destructive forces. Bright sunshine moments can disappear quickly. When darkness overtakes me, I find it hard to have clear thoughts.

My experiences can be likened to when night arrives. The darkness hides what I can normally see clearly in the daylight. My obstructed outlook needs God's enlightenment. I study the Holy Bible to learn how God wants me to conduct myself through my sorrowful situations.

As I have done so, my attitude about the troublesome circumstance changes. God provides contentment to make me strong in my weakness. With confident hope I look up to God who makes all things beautiful in His time. I consciously pursue God as He calms my troubled soul. I can rest in Him. He is my strength and help when I am discouraged.

My faith in Jesus Christ provides me hope of a great future to come. I keep my head up and look to Him who rescues me from the pit of despair. Jesus does this out of His great love for me as I trust Him.

Even when the sun turns to darkness, and the moon gives only a dull glow, God is faithful to see me through my difficult circumstances. He is my light in the chaotic world I live in.

HELPFUL PROMISES AND ENCOURAGEMENT WHEN DEPRESSED

"Only be strong and very courageous, being careful to do according to do all the law that Moses my servant commanded you. Do not turn from it to the right hand or to the left, that you may have good success wherever you go" Joshua 1:7.

"He regards the prayer of the destitute and does not despise their prayer" Psalm 102:17.

"Two are better than one, because they have a good reward for their toil. For if they fall, one will lift up his fellow. But woe to him who is alone when he falls and has not another to lift him up! Again, if two lie together, they keep warm, but how can one keep warm alone? And though a man might prevail against one who is alone, two will withstand him-a threefold cord is not quickly broken" Ecclesiastes 4:9-12.

"Like a swallow or a crane I chirp; I moan like a dove. My eyes are weary with looking upward. O Lord, I am oppressed; be my pledge of safety" Isaiah 38:14.

"So I went down to the potter's house, and there he was working at his wheel. And the vessel he was making of clay was spoiled in the potter's hand, and he reworked it into another vessel, as it seemed good to the potter to do" Jeremiah 18:3-4.

"Blessed be the God and Father of our Lord Jesus Christ, the Father of mercies and God of all comfort, who comforts us in all our affliction, so that we may be able to comfort those who are in any affliction, with the comfort with which we ourselves are comforted by God" 2 Corinthians 1:3-4.

"For at one time you were darkness, but now you are light in the Lord. Walk as children of light" Ephesians 5:8.

"So flee youthful passions and pursue righteousness, faith, love, and peace, along with those who call upon the Lord from a pure heart" 2 Timothy 2:22.

"Draw near to God, and he will draw near to you" James 4:8.

"Therefore let those who suffer according to God's will entrust their souls to a faithful Creator while doing good" 1 Peter 4:19.

CHAPTER 6
EVIL'S ROLE

"Put off your old self, which belongs to your former manner of
life and is corrupt through deceitful desires."
Ephesians 4:22

Karen and I prayed God would bless us with a child years
before Bonnie came into the world. From her first day on earth,
we kept her in our prayers. Our daughter lived a kind and
compassionate life. She honored God by doing what is right
and good.

We live in the physical realm, but there is also an unseen
spiritual world. Those who want to live for Jesus Christ need
His protection and help. The spiritual battle is real.

Near my desk I have a copy of Ron Dicianni's 1990
painting entitled *Spiritual Warfare*. The setting is at night. A
father kneels and prays for his child who is asleep in bed. A
large window in the background is framed in the shape of a
cross. The window is open to allow fresh air into the child's
bedroom. Outside the bedroom window is an angel in white
who fights off the powers of darkness as the father prays.

Evil forces are real, and influence everyone. Guardian angels do provide protection for those who trust Jesus.

The painting reminded me to pray for my daughter as she slept at night. I often prayed over Bonnie in the darkness. God answered my prayers. She seldom had bad dreams and enjoyed sound sleep.

Each morning, I read the Bible to her after breakfast. After reading we talked about how we could apply His Word to our lives. Then we prayed for the ability to honor Him in the day ahead.

My relationship with Jesus Christ is genuine. I wanted Bonnie to recognize how God would direct and defend her. God wants His followers to be aware of evil when it confronts them.

I ask Jesus daily to guide my thoughts and actions. The temptation to disobey God remains strong. My old self is still with me. My ungodly desires tempt me to draw away from God. I am always on guard against evil. I want Jesus to take charge of how I think and respond to others. Results are always better when I follow God instead of my own selfish desires.

Every night, before Bonnie went to sleep, we talked about how the morning devotional prepared us for our day. Bonnie learned to apply God's Word and appreciated His help in her life.

Bonnie knew the importance of a quiet time with God so she could learn from Him. The daily practice of Scripture reading, reflection and prayer became her own routine. As she did this, Bonnie reflected Christ through her life.

A PERSONAL FAITH IN GOD

From our daughter's infancy, Karen and I wanted Bonnie trust in Jesus Christ as her Savior. As our daughter grew, we often stopped to pray about a need or concern. No matter how big or small the issue, we wanted Bonnie to know God wants us to ask Him for His help when troubles arise.

One time as a preschool age child, Bonnie came into our house very disturbed. While playing outside, she realized she had lost a tiny Barbie doll shoe. Bonnie tried to find it but was unsuccessful.

A Barbie shoe is only a few millimeters in size. To find the tiny object outdoors appeared to be an impossible task. The lost shoe made my daughter very upset.

To help Bonnie settle down, Karen prayed with her. They asked Jesus to help them find the shoe. Then they went outside to look for it.

Karen asked Bonnie to think about where she had been. They followed the path Bonnie had taken and were able to find that tiny doll shoe. When they returned to the house, we rejoiced and again stopped to pray. We thanked God who cares about even the smallest details others might consider insignificant.

A decade later, as a teenager, Bonnie played the role of Cinderella's Fairy Godmother in her high school musical. The Godmother gave Cinderella a beautiful dress and a pair of glass shoes. Cinderella accidentally lost one of her special shoes at a dance and could not get it back.

Her true love, the prince, found the shoe, then used it to find Cinderella. At the end of the story Bonnie celebrated their reunion as she ended the musical with a song. Throughout her own life, Bonnie recognized that miracles happen every day.

Bonnie never forgot her Barbie doll shoe experience as a child. God's help to find the lost shoe provided a lasting memory when a greater challenge threatened her life.

Throughout her cancer journey, Bonnie never lost hope in God. She learned early to trust Him for what seemed to be impossible. Her confidence in Him never wavered. As Psalm 46:1 says, "God is our refuge and strength, a very present help in trouble."

THE FATHER'S HEART

As Bonnie's earthly father, I wanted my daughter to develop her own deep love for Jesus. She grew in faith as she developed her own close relationship with Him.

I noticed her love for God grow every day. She wanted to hear from God's Word and learned to memorize Scripture. Bonnie not only studied the Holy Bible, but she also applied His truths to her life.

As early as second grade, my daughter wanted others to know about her love for Jesus Christ. Her art teacher gave an assignment to make a repeat design. Bonnie drew three rows of four pink hearts horizontally. Inside each heart she placed a purple cross.

This simple drawing reflected Christ's love in her own heart. She lived in a such a way that Jesus could be seen in her behavior. Bonnie had a kind word for everyone. She showed kindness and respect to others.

From an early age my daughter picked up Christ's cross and died to herself. Bonnie did not physically die, but she learned to be content.

Bonnie patiently watched others celebrate their achievements. As Jesus says in Mark 9:35b, "If anyone would be first, he must be last of all and servant of all." I appreciated Bonnie's ability to place others before herself. She followed Christ's example. God rarely gets credit for the help He gives us.

Nevertheless, God holds no resentment, only gratification when others are blessed. Evil on the other hand, seeks to steal, kill and destroy what God originally created as very good. The battle between good and evil is recognizable to those who love God.

HAVE A PURE HEART

A pure heart requires a desire to honor God. Karen and I wanted to give our daughter a name to reflect God's character in her life.

Bonnie means beautiful. We prayed daily for God to develop a beautiful spirit in her. As she grew up others could see Him in the way she lived. Bonnie's middle name is Mae, which means great. We wanted her to do great things for God.

As her parents we wanted our daughter to live with a purpose. This happened as she developed a solid relationship with God.

Psalm 24:3-5 describes the result of obedience to God's Word. "Who shall ascend the hill of the LORD? And who shall stand in his holy place? He who has clean hands and a pure heart, who does not lift up his soul to what is false and does not swear deceitfully. He will receive blessing from the LORD and righteousness from the God of his salvation." God blesses those who obey Him.

As followers of Christ, Karen and I have experienced His presence with us. Bonnie's beautiful spirit helped to make our home a pleasant place to be. God continues to fill us with His joy as we live each day for Him.

Jesus told a parable about how everyone lives life on a wide road. However, God wants those who follow Him to live on His straight and narrow path. Jesus said in Matthew 7:13-14, "Enter by the narrow gate. For the gate is wide and the way is easy that leads to destruction, and those who enter by it are many. For the gate is narrow and the way is hard that leads to life, and those who find it are few."

As a family, we intentionally renew our minds and trust Christ. We encourage one another daily to stay faithful to God and live according to His Word.

As a follower of Jesus Christ my ambition is to allow Him to change my old self-centered ways. My perspective changes when I remember, God's ways are much different than my own.

My family has gone against the destructive flow of this world. We recognize evil forces that cause disharmony and tempt us to disobey God.

EVIL DESTROYS

Evil is a powerful force. Intense wickedness takes my attention off of God. Evil often takes me by surprise. The way of God is good, but wrongdoing is destructive. As Romans 6:23 says, "For the wages of sin is death, but the free gift of God is eternal life in Christ Jesus our Lord."

Bad influences can deceive me as a follower of Christ. When I disobey God's Word, my thoughts are separated from the life-giving message of Jesus.

Galatians 5:17 reminds me, "For the desires of the flesh are against the Spirit, and the desires of the Spirit are against the flesh, for these are opposed to each other, to keep you from doing the things you want to do." I know I am in a spiritual battle when my desires are not in line with God's Word.

From the beginning of creation, Satan's goal has been to deceive people. When I believe his lies, my mind gets corrupted, and I am led astray from God's truth. When I am deceived, I do what is wrong.

When Bonnie went through her cancer, and after her death, I experienced many intense frustrations. Doubts arose about God's goodness. Discouragement, despair, and discontentment were constant problems for me. With the help of the Holy Spirit, I have been able to fight the forces of evil and obey God.

I intentionally remind myself to depend on Jesus. My irreversible circumstances have made me realize He is my strength. No one, nor any temporary sedative, could provide the long-term inner change that I needed when Bonnie died.

Only Jesus Christ has the ability to break the power of evil and protect me from harmful thoughts of hopelessness. My despair and confusion caused me to ask for His help.

James 1:5 reminds me, "If any of you lacks wisdom, let him ask God, who gives generously to all without reproach, and it will be given him." God helps me when I am weak and disappointed. God gives me His wisdom when I ask for help and do not know what to do.

I am thankful Jesus is always with me. He gives me strength in my weakness. He helps me stay on the straight and narrow path.

Satan wants to destroy my faith in God. Yet the Holy Spirit protects and comforts me in my spiritual battles. When I get hurt and disappointed, God's Holy Spirit always reminds me I am never alone in my fight against evil.

SENSITIVITY TO EVIL

My family and I have traveled through many different towns, cities, and countries. As we passed through some places on our journeys, Karen and Bonnie often felt a strong awareness of evil oppression.

Karen describes evil oppression as an overpowering feeling of darkness. I recognize evil when it is displayed in immoral behavior, such as when people behave in ways known to be against God's Word. Their uncontrollable actions enslave them.

Throughout my life, I have observed how evil can impact and control a person's thoughts and actions. Ephesians 6:12 tells us there are many evil forces in the world. These evil powers influence people to do what is wrong.

I often recognize evil in nice, clean, and interesting places. Many of these locations are historic sites where extremely cruel wickedness happened in the past.

An evil spirit can remain in a place where ungodly acts previously occurred. From a human perspective, past evil events are sometimes viewed as entertainment, such as haunted houses or ghost walks. On the other hand, from a spiritual perspective, I recognize how evil influenced what happened. The consequences of wickedness are awful.

Karen and Bonnie's sensitivity to evil made me more aware of spiritual forces at some places we visited. Upon closer examination of an environment, I am also able to discern an evil spirit. Even though many view the same place as harmless fun. Evil should never be accepted as good. We must recognize how it affects us.

First John 3:8 reminds me, "Whoever makes a practice of sinning is of the devil, for the devil has been sinning from the beginning. The reason the Son of God appeared was to destroy the works of the devil." From the time of Adam and Eve, people have been under the curse of sin.

Thankfully, Jesus came to liberate everyone from sin. We all need His forgiveness and restoration. My salvation in Jesus Christ has given me an awareness of spiritual powers. Therefore, I make the effort to protect myself and my family from the forces of evil.

EVIL CLOSE TO HOME

After a six-month furlough in America, my family encountered an unexpected evil presence in our African home. Since another family needed our former home during our absence, we moved to a different house.

The large building once served as a medical clinic for a religious group who were not Christians. Our encounters with evil spirits in the building were both creepy and unnatural.

One bothersome manifestation involved a door which banged throughout the night. A warped door frame caused the door not to fit properly, so it would not close. The unusual movement of the door never happened in the daylight hours.

Every night I checked to see if there was a breeze which caused the door to swing freely. Each examination revealed no air movement to cause the door to bang by itself all night long.

I tried to brace the door with a heavy chair, but at dawn I always found the chair moved away from the door. Not even a solid wooden chair could keep the door from banging throughout the night.

This happened years before the use of security cameras. However, even if the door could have been filmed through the night, it is unlikely the spiritual force would have been seen. An evil spirit is often not seen by the natural eye. Evil can be recognized by its unnatural, oppressive, and disruptive power.

I realized this one morning when I found my Bible on the floor face down underneath a coffee table. I always place my Bible on a table or bookshelf face up. I make every effort to handle the Holy Bible with respect since it is God's Word.

Karen and I recognized the evil influence in our home. With the help of other strong believers in Christ, we prayed throughout the house. We audibly called upon Jesus to remove all evil forces from the building. We invited Jesus into every area of our home. We wanted His presence of peace to be with us in this house.

James 2:19 says demons believe in Jesus Christ and fear Him. The name of Jesus casts out demonic forces. This is also recorded in Luke 4:34 where the spirit of an unclean demon said, "'Ha! What have you to do with us, Jesus of Nazareth? Have you come to destroy us? I know who you are – the Holy One of God.'"

Even after the group prayed through our house, we continued to be disturbed by evil spirits in the building. Spiritual powers are very strong. This experience taught me how a determined effort is necessary to overcome evil.

Confirmation of the strong evil force in this residence reappeared when a medical doctor came to visit us with his dog. After several attempts to order his dog into our home, the doctor realized his dog sensed the evil spirits inside the building. Neither our friend nor his dog wanted to stay, and they departed.

Another group of people came to pray through our house a second time. Thankfully the strange occurrences finally ceased. As Psalm 28:6-7 says, "Blessed be the LORD! For he has heard the voice of my pleas for mercy. The LORD is my strength and my shield; in him my heart trusts, and I am helped."

While we lived in that house God placed a special protection around our daughter. She did not know about the strange events and slept soundly each night. However, after a month we were able to move back to our former home. Karen and I were finally able to sleep again.

BE NOT OVERCOME

The outcome of our hardship could appear as if evil is more powerful than God. We learned the truth of Psalm 94:22. "But the LORD has become my stronghold, and my God the rock of my refuge."

We prayed for a certain conclusion, but the result did not happen as quickly as we anticipated. Throughout Scripture, there are examples of unforeseen natural and spiritual events which can affect a person for life. At times, bad circumstances and evil forces can seem to be victorious over us as believers in God.

However, in the end, God will have the victory. By trusting in God, the situation for my family improved. After we resettled into our old home, we felt more secure and content. The evil we experienced upon our return to Africa no longer impacted us, and God protected us from further evil influences.

Psalm 91:9 reminds me, "Because you have made the LORD your dwelling place—the Most High, who is my refuge —no evil shall be allowed to befall you, no plague come near your tent." My temporary home here on earth was made safe through God's protective care.

From my travels to different places, I have observed how some parts of the world have strong territorial spirits. I have seen how charms and spiritual idols can cause destructive harm. I am careful to keep items out of my home that are associated with ungodly influences.

When an object has evil power associated with it, the object has potential to harm me. Evil tries to keep me away from God. When I allow external forces to influence me, their destructive power can impact my life.

BE CAREFUL OF EVIL INFLUENCES

Satan is clever in the way he leads us away from God. He frequently does his work through addictions. An attraction into unhealthy lifestyles deceives vulnerable victims to be unwittingly enslaved to bad situations.

When I came to faith in Christ, I realized the rock music I enjoyed conflicted with God's Word. I had listened to such loud music that my ear drums were constantly ringing. It was hard to hear God's "still small voice" when my ears were damaged from the noise of this world.

The songs did not allow me to be attentive to God's amazing beauty around me. Instead, God felt distant as I disengaged from my faith with the restless music. What I listened to influenced me to miss out on God's purpose for my life.

Repetitive messages of hopelessness filled my mind with temptations to rebel against God. Instead of mindful praise and thankfulness to God, my life craved unwholesome desires. This eventually led me to throw several hundred classic rock albums into the trash.

Some people thought I should have sold them to make some money. When a destructive influence is recognized, the evil item should be destroyed. As a believer in Jesus Christ, I gave Him total control of my life. I did not want to tempt others to turn away from God as I had.

Acts 19:18-19 tells how occult books were burned when people received Jesus as their Savior. The market price of those books totaled 50,000 pieces of silver, over five million dollars at today's cash value. Even if a financial loss occurs to eliminate evil influences, God rewards those who trust Him.

Jesus told His disciples in Mark 8:36, "For what does it profit a man to gain the whole world and forfeit his soul?" I experienced true life in Christ. He took away my old habits which once led me into a dead-end life.

Pornographic materials were also a destructive influence on my life. I made an intentional effort not to fill my mind with immoral thoughts and discarded those images. Jesus says in

Matthew 5:27-28, "You have heard that it was said, 'You shall not commit adultery.' But I say to you that everyone who looks at a woman with lustful intent has already committed adultery with her in his heart."

Porn is not just an adult issue but is also a problem for children. At a young age I got exposed to graphic materials. I could not safeguard my mind from ungodly thoughts and behavior. When my mind gets affected by evil thoughts, I am easily motivated to do what is wrong.

I needed to daily remind myself about my identity in Jesus Christ. My value and beauty as an individual are given to me by God. He created me, and His love has given me life. His Word assures me He is faithful to overcome evil. Through the help of His Spirit in me, I live my life for Him as He intends.

Alcohol is another addictive influence I have chosen to avoid in my life. There is a reason why liquor stores refer to their strong drinks as spirits. When I abused and misused alcohol, there were ungodly spirits who were able to control my thoughts and actions. God's Spirit was suppressed when I permitted alcohol to influence my thoughts and behavior.

When I studied for my Master of Arts in Counseling degree, I observed an autopsy. The medical doctor took note of the man's liver. Instead of a healthy red liver, it had turned bright yellow. This revealed that he was an alcoholic.

The autopsy reminds me how I too could have fallen into a life of alcoholism, if it were not for Christ's powerful work in my life. Jesus provides me contentment, comfort, and confidence so I now have no need to drink alcohol to enjoy life.

A RELATIONSHIP WITH CHRIST

Life gets difficult when circumstances dishearten me. Thankfully Jesus daily confirms and reveals that He is my light in a spiritually darkened world. Evil spirits are actively at work to discourage and deceive me. I am grateful how the Holy Spirit guides my thoughts when tempted by the deception of selfish desires.

I never used a Ouija board but have observed others who used it. They engage with a spiritual force they believe will predict their future. This is an activity people must avoid. Evil spirits actively deceive people in order to control them. The Ouija board puts people in spiritual bondage as they communicate with ungodly spirits.

First Corinthians 2:14-16 says, "The natural person does not accept the things of the Spirit of God, for they are folly to him, and he is not able to understand them because they are spiritually discerned. The spiritual person judges all things, but is himself to be judged by no one. 'For who has understood the mind of the Lord so as to instruct him?' But we have the mind of Christ."

People who do not love Jesus Christ with their entire heart neither seek Him nor know God. His instructions sound foolish to them. Nonetheless, as I apply God's Word to my life, Christ transforms me into His image.

A virtual reality player is another way I could be influenced to escape reality. A virtual reality mask is placed over the eyes to see artificial images. The likeness appears to be authentic, but it is only an image in a person's mind. Valuable time is wasted when I focus on what is not true through entertainment devices.

God wants me to put off my old self and renew my mind through the Bible. His Word refreshes me. The reality and certainty of Scripture confirm God's timeless truths. My distress is overcome when I obey Him.

Second Corinthians 5:17 says, "Therefore, if anyone is in Christ, he is a new creation. The old has passed away; behold, the new has come." Jesus has made me a new creation. I have been born again!

I am grateful God does not leave me alone to fight the battle against evil on my own. Jesus defeated all evil when he died on the cross. When Jesus resurrected from the dead, He made it possible for me to know Him and experience His presence with me. As I daily develop my relationship with Jesus, God is gracious to reveal Himself to me through the Holy Spirit. I am indeed blessed by God.

AN UNEXPECTED DISCOVERY

After my daughter died, I knew a change needed to happen in my life. I could continue to be depressed, angry, unhappy, and discontent, or I could allow God to transform me.

Satan is not equal to God because he is a created being. Satan is not all-knowing, nor all-powerful. He certainly is able to cause confusion and division, but he can never overrule God.

God has placed limits on what Satan can do. The first two chapters in the book of Job explain this fact.

Satan and his demons can have a powerful impact. This is because God gives everyone free will. I have the freedom to choose between good and evil. Scripture reminds me that I can forsake God and do what is wrong. When I do wrong, I sin against God. I have learned disobedience against God never satisfies me.

Thankfully God has given me the awareness of evil forces who want to control and abuse me. To overcome these forces, I must be obedient to His Word and be alert to the spiritual darkness around me.

Prayer, faith, and steadfastness in the Scriptures help me to stay confident when evil forces cause me to doubt God. I am also grateful for how the Holy Spirit guards me against evil. He keeps my mind set upon God's Word.

HELPFUL PROMISES AND ENCOURAGEMENT WHEN RESISTING EVIL

"Do not enter the path of the wicked, and do not walk in the way of evil. Avoid it; do not go on it; turn away from it and pass on" Proverbs 4:14-15.

"Woe to those who call evil good and good evil, who put darkness for light and light for darkness, who put bitter for sweet and sweet for bitter!" Isaiah 5: 20.

"The eye is the lamp of the body. So if your eye is healthy, your whole body will be full of light, but if your eye is bad, your whole body will be full of darkness. If then the light in you is darkness, how great is the darkness!" Matthew 6:22-23.

"For although they knew God, they did not honor him as God or give thanks to him, but they became futile in their thinking, and their foolish hearts were darkened" Romans 1:21.

"In their case the god of this world has blinded the minds of unbelievers, to keep them from seeing the light of the gospel of the glory of Christ, who is the image of God" 2 Corinthians 4:4.

"But the Lord is faithful. He will establish you and guard you against the evil one" 2 Thessalonians 3:3.

"Since therefore the children share in flesh and blood, he himself likewise partook of the same things, that through death he might destroy the one who has the power of death, that is the devil, and deliver all those who through the fear of death were subject to lifelong slavery" Hebrews 2:14-15.

"Be sober minded; be watchful. Your adversary the devil prowls around like a roaring lion, seeking someone to devour. Resist him, firm in your faith, knowing that the same kinds of suffering are being experienced by your brotherhood throughout the world. And after you have suffered a little while, the God of all grace, who has called you to his eternal glory in Christ, will himself restore, confirm, strengthen, and establish you" 1 Peter 5: 8-10.

CHAPTER 7
GOD'S ROLE

"The LORD is good to all, and his mercy is over all that he has
made."
Psalm 145:9

The autumn after Bonnie died, I planted daffodil bulbs at her
grave site. The following spring, I went to the cemetery and
found them in bloom. I rejoiced to see new life come out of the
ground where she is buried.

I looked at the daffodils and noticed a few blooms had died.
I bent over to "deadhead" the decayed flowers. Immediately,
my lower back jolted in great pain. I never had such intense
pain in my life.

This occurred at a terrible moment. The next day Karen
and I were scheduled to travel to Jerusalem for a three-week
study tour. After that, we would spend two weeks in Jordan to
visit biblical sites.

My intense pain gave me doubts about our anticipated
adventure. Thankfully, God calmed my mind, body, and soul

about my pilgrimage. He assured me He would strengthen me and be my help to endure the journey.

A PILGRIMAGE VERSUS A RETREAT

Karen and I always wanted to visit the Holy Land. I was determined to travel with my pain as I did not have any prescription pain killers for my troublesome condition.

I spoke with a medical doctor friend about my injury before I departed. He advised me to cancel my trip and see my primary doctor as soon as possible. In the meantime, he wanted me to get plenty of bedrest.

If I were on a retreat, I would have followed his directions. A retreat is when a person withdraws from everyday activities to find rest, quietness, and renewal. However, I intended my Holy Land journey to be a pilgrimage.

A pilgrimage is an intentional desire to reach an important place for reflection and appreciation. I intended to fly from United States to Israel, then see the biblical sites mentioned in the Holy Bible. The journey gave me an opportunity to deepen my love for God, and the land He describes in Scripture.

The five-week pilgrimage physically challenged me. If I were in my normal state of health the journey would have been no problem. However, by the conclusion of the physically intensive five weeks, I struggled to endure because of my painful affliction.

As the pilgrimage neared the end I slept on the edge of my bed. I could not lift my legs to get them into bed. Karen had to pick them up for me. Each morning Karen took my arm and pulled me up out of bed. She had to put my socks and shoes on me, then helped me get upright. My desire and excitement to see biblical landmarks kept me motivated and determined to keep up with the group.

I trusted God to get me through each day. Most people in my condition would have been under close medical care. Instead, God allowed me to complete my journey.

Most of the group I traveled with were young people who came as students. Lectures focused on the historical and geographical importance of the sites we visited.

Not everyone knew about my inability to move easily. Several students encouraged and supported me in my affliction. Some intentionally lingered behind so others would not see my pain.

ENTRANCE INTO JERUSALEM

A favorite memory of mine as a young boy occurred at church on Palm Sunday. I lived in an area where no palm trees grew. When I received a palm leaf, it reminded me of a place far different from my home.

I liked the firm texture of the palm leaf. When I got home from church, my mother bent the leaf into a cross. The cross is a reminder of Christ's sacrifice when He gave His life for me.

When I entered the old city of Jerusalem, the account of Christ's triumphal entry, where people laid palm branches before Him, came to life. My pain faded for a moment as I experienced the reality of a long-desired hope to be in the Holy Land.

Karen and I first flew into Tel Aviv, then took a taxi to Jerusalem. When we arrived, our driver dropped us off outside the Jaffa Gate. The Jaffa Gate is the busiest of the seven gates of the Old City of Jerusalem.

Thankfully, a person with a small wooden cart picked up our suitcases and took us to our hotel. We needed to walk up a gentle slope along a hillside before we passed through the Jaffa

Gate to reach our hotel. This western passage into old Jerusalem is located near the top of Mount Zion.

Nearby is the upper room where Christ's last supper is believed to have taken place. On the lower floor, Jewish people pray where King David is thought to be buried. Ancient history of biblical events immediately became real and alive in a fresh new way.

A narrow path goes to the Jaffa Gate. The pathway is outside a fortress wall. A tall tower built in 1655 gives the Citadel an Islamic appearance. Yet part of the fortification is from the Roman occupation when King Herod ruled in Jerusalem.

So, the Citadel may be where Herod asked the wisemen to inform him where Christ could be found. Herod wanted no other King but himself. He wanted to murder God's Son who was born as the King of kings in Bethlehem.

Three decades after King Herod, Pilate could have sentenced Jesus to death at the Citadel. I found it fascinating how both the wisemen's visit and Christ's trial may have occurred at the same place.

Both Herod and Pilate gave an order to end the life of Jesus Christ. Their lives are long gone, but Jesus is still alive and well as He works through His people here on earth.

The political leaders of Rome are no longer near the fortress. This place, where important decisions were once made for the people of Jerusalem and citizens of the Holy Land, remains an important historic site.

Thousands of people daily pass through the Jaffa Gate, but no trash litters the ground. I beheld architecture constructed centuries ago, yet still beautiful and as strong as the day they were built.

I did not expect Jerusalem would produce such awe in me. Even the walkways made of white stone caught my attention.

The stones are well-worn by millions of pilgrims who have walked on these same stones for centuries. I also walked where Jesus gave His life for me.

THE PILGRIMAGE HIGHLIGHTS

Bonnie's death occurred two years before my Holy Land visit. I had never been to Israel before, but my study of Scripture put a deep desire in me to experience the land where God did miraculous works. While in the promised land I prayed for God to open my eyes to see what He wanted me to discover.

One unexpected discovery occurred in the Judaean wilderness near the Dead Sea. An archaeological find in 1947 at Qumran reminded me how God safeguards His Word.

Scrolls were found in old pottery jars. Every book of the Old Testament, except Esther, was found. This confirms the fact God's Word is inerrant and without fault.

I had the chance to closely examine a few scrolls in a museum in Jerusalem. They had been hidden in caves for nearly two thousand years but are now publicly displayed at the Israel Museum in the "Shrine of the Book."

I am grateful the Scriptures provide me with a firm foundation. The scrolls once in clay pots are the same Scriptures I study in the Holy Bible. This reminds me when life gets dark, God's Word remains my source of hope.

The Holy Bible is His Word as Revelation 21:5 says, "And he who was seated on the throne said, 'Behold, I am making all things new.' Also he said, 'Write this down, for these words are trustworthy and true.'" First Peter 1:25 also says, "'but the word of the Lord remains forever.' And this word is the good news that was preached to you." I thank God for His Good News that has changed my life.

THE WAY OF SUFFERING

A famous Street in Jerusalem is the Via Dolorosa which means "the way of sorrow." Along this narrow road is Saint Anne's Church. Crusaders built the church several hundred years after Christ carried His cross down this road.

On the grounds of Saint Anne's Church are ruins known as the pools of Bethesda. The pools originally held water for Jewish pilgrims who worshipped God at the Temple. Thousands of people once used the water while they walked along the road known today as the Via Dolorosa.

John 5:1-15 mentions how water at one pool occasionally stirred unexpectedly. Many people who needed physical healing stayed close to the pool, because the first person who entered the pool when the water stirred recovered from their physical ailment.

A man who could not walk sat by the pool for more than thirty years. When the water moved unexpectedly, others always reached the pool before he could enter the water. Then one day Jesus asked the lame man if he wanted to be healed.

The man told Jesus how others reached the pool before he could. Jesus told him to stand and pick up his mat. With no additional questions the man stood up and walked away.

Today the pools of Bethesda are dry, empty foundations of rock. They reminded me of my sorrowful condition. Like the paralyzed man, my physical pain caused me to struggle down the Via Dolorosa.

No one ever suffered the pain Jesus experienced when He died. His sacrifice on the cross restored me. I am grateful how Jesus daily gives me needed strength to get through my hardships.

As Hebrews 12:12-13 reminds me, "Therefore lift your drooping hands and strengthen your weak knees, and make straight paths for your feet, so that what is lame may not be put out of joint but rather be healed." God uses my weaknesses so I can receive His restoration in my life.

Ephesians 6:10 emphasizes, "Finally, be strong in the Lord and in the strength of his might." After decades of obedience to Christ as my Savior, I have learned God is the ultimate source of my strength.

UNEXPECTED MIRACLES

After John the Baptist's arrest, Jesus departed his childhood home in Nazareth and lived in Capernaum. The town is located about seventy miles north of Jerusalem.

Jesus did not have His own house, so He often stayed at the home of Simon Peter. Matthew 8:14-15 recalled what happened in Capernaum, "And when Jesus entered Peter's house, he saw his mother-in-law lying sick with a fever. He touched her hand, and the fever left her, and she rose and began to serve him."

While in Capernaum I thought about what happens when a miracle occurs. A supernatural healing cannot be explained by science.

My body is far too complex to have randomly evolved over millions of years. Jesus merely touched a person, or spoke His Word to an individual in need, and a powerful change happened in them. Historical sites all around the Sea of Galilee reminded me of His miracles.

These places recalled how Jesus defies the laws of nature. As I asked Him to remove my emotional and physical pain, He reminded me how God has already restored my hopeless condition. He unexpectedly transformed my life through His Son Jesus Christ when He saved me.

RISEN FROM THE DEAD

Prior to my decision to fully follow Jesus Christ, I lived like a dead man. I could not break the bondage of my prideful self-centered nature that kept me from God.

Ephesians 2:1-2 describes my former condition, "And you were dead in the trespasses and sins in which you once walked, following the course of this world, following the prince of the power of the air, the spirit that is now at work in the sons of disobedience."

My inability to live as God desires left me unhappy and hopeless. I lived like a dead man who is not able to be free of fear. Doubts and insecurity about myself troubled me.

Thankfully Jesus Christ has set me free from my self-centered bondage. Ever since I invited Jesus into my life, He has provided me the Holy Spirit. He enables me to discern what God declares is right, then helps me to obey His Word.

The result of Christ's sacrifice is made known in 1 Corinthians 15:56-57. "The sting of death is sin, and the power of sin is the law. But thanks be to God, who gives us the victory through our Lord Jesus Christ."

Jesus Christ took my sin upon Himself when He died on the cross. Through Him I am now able to live free from the curse of sin. This does not mean I have no difficulties to overcome. But I am able to deal with my problems with God's help.

Every day I trust Jesus to empower me with His strength. He knows my struggle to change my self-centered behavior. Therefore, I do as 1 Peter 5:6-7 says, "Humble yourselves, therefore, under the mighty hand of God so at the proper time he may exalt you, casting all your anxieties on him, because he cares for you."

The Holy Spirit also reassures me how God makes things

right in His time. When Jesus died, it appeared as if evil had triumphed over Christ, but three days later He rose from the dead.

I used to think that life went from birth to death. However, Christ's death and resurrection have given me eternal life with Him. This earthly life is only the beginning of a greater life yet to come.

Just as God resurrected His crucified Son Jesus Christ back to life, He has promised to raise me up one day to be with Him in heaven.

This world is my temporary home. As Philippians 3:20-21 says, "But our citizenship is in heaven, and from it we await a Savior, the Lord Jesus Christ, who will transform our lowly body to be like his glorious body, by the power that enables him even to subject all things to himself."

INSIGHT FROM THE SITES

There are two locations where Christ's death and resurrection are thought to have occurred. One is the Church of the Holy Sepulcher, and the other is the Garden Tomb.

The most noticeable observation at each location is an empty tomb. Jesus Christ physically rose from the dead and is alive today! His resurrection has changed my life as I live for Him every day.

My visit to the Church of the Holy Sepulcher had a powerful impact upon me. In 325 AD Emperor Constantine the Great ordered a stone structure built near the Via Dolorosa. A large rotunda covers the tomb of Jesus. The roof also protects a rock formation considered to be where Christ died on a cross.

Rome destroyed Jerusalem in 70 AD. The city lay in ruins for 250 years. First century Christians were scattered from

Jerusalem and persecuted for their faith. First century believers were unable to maintain the area where Christ's death and resurrection took place.

Constantine had Golgotha cleared of dirt and rock piles left behind from the Roman destruction two centuries earlier. Today a large white stone with a deep indent and a large crack are revered as a place where Christ may have died on the cross. Matthew 27:51 records how the ground shook and rocks split when Jesus died.

Under the large rotunda is a small marble building. Inside is a stone altar where Christ is believed to have been buried. In 1808 AD a fire badly damaged the Church of the Holy Sepulcher. War in Europe kept western attention off the disaster.

After the fire, the Greek Orthodox Church made needed repairs at the Church of the Holy Sepulcher. This is why the surroundings around Christ's grave site have an Eastern Orthodox appearance.

Only a few people at a time can enter Christ's empty tomb at the church. A few candles around a stone altar light up the dark space. A great joy came upon me in the unoccupied burial place. No remains of Christ's body were there because of His resurrection.

The words of 1 Corinthians 15:42-44 tell me I have a natural body, and a spiritual body. "So is it with the resurrection of the dead. What is sown is perishable; what is raised is imperishable. It is sown in dishonor; it is raised in glory. It is sown in weakness; it is raised in power. It is sown a natural body; it is raised a spiritual body." As a believer in Jesus Christ, I have been raised to new life.

The truth and reality of Christ's empty grave flooded my soul with great joy. Jesus rose from the dead and lives! Everyone who believes in Him is promised eternal life with God. He has prepared a home for all His followers.

Before Karen and I departed the tomb we prayed. We gave thanks to Jesus for all He has done for us. He has given us new life, not only here on earth, but in the life yet to come with Him in heaven.

A few days later, Karen and I visited the Garden Tomb, located a few blocks away from the Church of the Holy Sepulcher. My painful back limited my movement, but I walked from my hotel near the Jaffa Gate to visit the Garden Tomb. Most of the biblical sites in the old city of Jerusalem are close to each other and can be easily reached by foot.

On a hillside near the Garden Tomb gravesite is a rocky cliff. The rock slope has two indents near the top of its hillside. Underneath the shallow caves is a large rock. It sticks out from the cliffside.

The rock formation gives the appearance of a human skull. This rock formation may be what is described in Matthew 27:33.

The Garden Tomb gravesite is large. Unlike the Church of the Holy Sepulcher tomb, six or seven adults can comfortably stand inside the Garden Tomb. The Garden Tomb is confirmed to be from the first century. Scripture teaches a rich man named Joseph of Arimathea placed Jesus into a tomb cut out of rock. Only a wealthy person could afford such an expensive grave.

The doorway of Christ's tomb required a large stone to seal the entrance. A massive rock covered the way into Christ's grave. This distinctive feature is easily seen at this tomb.

Today, the Garden Tomb Association based in London takes care of the grounds. This special place provided me another opportunity to reflect on Christ's resurrection and His love for me. The Garden Tomb is an example of a grave from the time of Christ.

The easy accessibility of these grave sites reminded me of

how I can come before Him at any time. Hebrews 4:16 encourages believers to approach God with assurance, "Let us then with confidence draw near to the throne of grace, that we may receive mercy and find grace to help in time of need."

I am thankful Christ's death and resurrection made me right with God. The empty tomb is confirmation that He physically rose from death to life.

Without Christ's forgiveness I am doomed to live a life in spiritual darkness. Jesus enables me to literally see His awesome presence as I read the Holy Bible, and marvel at His creation.

The sites of Christ's sacrifice gave me insight, and a great appreciation for His salvation. His death and resurrection provided me a right relationship with my Almighty Creator. Without Him I would be doomed to a life of spiritual darkness and despair.

STOPPED AT THE WALL

On the first night of my Holy Land pilgrimage, I had the privilege to pray at the Wailing Wall. Karen and I went with our study group. We quietly walked through dimly lit and narrow passageways of old Jerusalem, then suddenly entered a large, brightly lit courtyard.

Flood lights made the Western Wall shine. The darkness of night could not hide such an incomparable site. When we arrived, few people were in the courtyard. I had an immediate desire to worship God.

This is a place of honor and respect to God. Men are instructed to go to the left and women to the right. I was given a small cap, or kippah, to cover my head. I was excited to enter this very special place.

When I placed my hands on the wall, I realized this is the western foundation of God's Temple, where Christ Himself went to worship His heavenly Father.

Even though my back screamed in pain, my heavy heart ached more because of my daughter's death. Yet I stood in awe before God. This holy place revealed God's greatness to me.

I beheld the same foundation where God forgave the sins of His people, and where Christ's earthly parents dedicated Him to His heavenly Father. I constantly looked up to God with great humility as I prayed at the Western Wall.

A small bush grew between the cracks in the stones on the wall above me. The bush served as a reminder for me to hold on to God and trust Him for His provision.

After I finished praying, I began to leave when a Jewish man invited me into his synagogue, located just left of the Western Wall. No one else from my group got invited, but I could not pass up his invitation.

I had never been in a synagogue, but this particular house of worship included the Western Wall. This is where King Herod reconstructed the Temple foundation before the birth of Christ.

I entered the synagogue where Jewish men humbly prayed. They worshiped God in quiet reverence. The Western Wall before us served as a reminder that we stood on holy ground, a place where God revealed Himself.

I wanted to see more of their synagogue, but I knew my wife and tour group would be concerned if I did not return. No one knew I had gone into the synagogue.

Before I left the synagogue, I told the Jewish man about my daughter's death. With tears in his eyes, he gave me a small candle. I went to the Western Wall in darkness, but departed with a source of light, and the blessing of a new friend.

RECEIVED JUST AS I AM

The next day, a tour guide informed my group about a strict dress code at places of worship in Israel. What he said shocked me. I had been invited into a synagogue the night before wearing a casual shirt, shorts, and hiking shoes. That was not proper dress for a synagogue.

Then I thought about 1 Samuel 16:7, "For the LORD sees not as man sees: man looks on the outward appearance, but the LORD looks on the heart." So also, my Jewish friend looked beyond my informal garments and recognized me as someone who loves God.

At the pool of Bethesda, I remembered Christ's ability to heal and strengthen a lame man who trusted Him. Jesus touched him and gave him supernatural strength to walk. Christ's presence continues to strengthen me today.

When I visited the possible sites of Christ's crucifixion and resurrection, the thought of His salvation revitalized my heart. I left each place with inexpressible joy. He died and rose again to make me right with God.

While at the Western Wall, I admired the greatness of God. His undeserved acceptance of me in my sad, broken, and desperate condition enabled me to receive unexpected blessings.

When I went into the Western Wall Synagogue, I entered improperly dressed, but no one looked at me in a way to indicate I was not welcomed. I joined my Jewish friends as a fellow worshiper and believer in the God of Abraham, Isaac, and Jacob.

Even in a dark, dirty cave in Qumran my soul gave thanks for God's goodness. He preserved the Bible for thousands of years in fragile clay pots to remind me His Word is incapable of error. He also keeps watch over me in my weakness.

Throughout my pilgrimage I recognized my fragile condition, and God's ability to mold me. A clay pot can be broken, but as long as the clay remains soft, the potter is able to reshape it. Therefore, I daily trust God to shape me into His image.

God made it possible for me to complete my five-week pilgrimage through the Holy Land. He provided kind companions who knew about my struggles, and they encouraged me to complete the journey.

Upon my return to the United States, I received physical therapy. I learned my pain did not occur because of a spine injury, but a pulled hamstring. More than six months of intensive physical therapy passed before I could walk effortlessly again.

My physical pain eventually went away, and God continues to repair my broken heart. I trust in Him to daily restore me. I have experienced God's love in a powerful way. My renewed life in Him motivates me to respect, admire, fear, and praise my Almighty God on a daily basis.

HELPFUL PROMISES AND ENCOURAGEMENT WHEN IN DISTRESS

"Behold, to the LORD your God belong heaven and the heaven of heavens, the earth with all that is in it" Deuteronomy 10:14.

"The Lord is my shepherd; I shall not want. He makes me lie down in green pastures. He leads me beside still waters. He restores my soul. He leads me in paths of righteousness for his name's sake. Even though I walk through the valley of the shadow of death, I will fear no evil, for you are with me; your rod and your staff, they comfort me" Psalm 23:1-4.

"Have you not known? Have you not heard? The LORD is the everlasting God, the Creator of the ends of the earth. He does not faint or grow weary; his understanding is unsearchable. He gives power to the faint, and to him who has no might he increases strength. Even youths shall faint and be weary, and young men shall fall exhausted; but they who wait for the Lord shall renew their strength; they shall mount up with wings like eagles; they shall run and not be weary; they shall walk and not faint" Isaiah 40:28-31.

"For I know the plans I have for you, declares the LORD, plans for welfare and not for evil, to give you a future and a hope. Then you will call upon me and come and pray to me, and I will hear you. You will seek me and find me, when you seek me with all your heart" Jeremiah 29:11-13.

"He has told you, O man, what is good: and what does the LORD require of you but to do justice, and to love kindness, and to walk humbly with your God?" Micah 6:8.

"Or which one of you, if his son asks him for bread, will give him a stone? Or if he asks for a fish, will give him a serpent? If you then, who are evil, know how to give good gifts to your children, how much more will your Father who is in heaven give good things to those who ask him!" Matthew 7:9-11.

"Now we have received not the spirit of the world, but the Spirit who is from God, that we might understand the things freely given us by God" 1 Corinthians 2:12.

"For by him all things were created, in heaven and on earth, visible and invisible, whether thrones or dominions or rulers or authorities—all things were created through him and for him. And he is before all things, and in him all things hold together" Colossians 1:16-17.

CHAPTER 8

REPENTANCE

"I am reminded of your sincere faith, a faith that dwelt first in your grandmother Lois and your mother Eunice and now, I am sure, dwells in you as well."

2 Timothy 1:5

I frequently think about my daughter's sincere faith in God. Her genuine devotion reminds me of her deep love for God. Bonnie lived each day with a steadfast confidence in Him.

At her funeral, a high school teacher spoke about Bonnie's trust in God. The instructor observed her life and recognized the beauty of Christ in her.

The teacher compared Bonnie's outlook on life to virgin Mary's response after she received a divine message from God. Her reply is known as the Magnificat. "My soul magnifies the Lord, and my spirit rejoices in God my Savior, for He has looked on the humble estate of his servant" (Luke 1:46-48).

Like Mary, Bonnie wanted to do what God desired for her life. She served Him daily with a deep appreciation for how He used her life.

My daughter's teachers were dumbfounded how at the end of each class she never failed to tell them, "Thank you." They told Bonnie it was not necessary, but she enjoyed expressing appreciation, especially to those who showed their concern for her.

Three recognizable traits Bonnie displayed were thankfulness, gentleness, and contentment. Her life was far from perfect, but the ability to spontaneously and naturally be grateful came from her heart.

Out of her genuine desire to live for God, she reflected His love. God's joy always shined brightly through her life. Even in difficult situations Bonnie maintained a positive outlook.

While Bonnie went through difficult days of cancer, she invariably expressed gratitude. Bonnie seldom focused on herself. Her heart desire aimed to encourage and build up others.

My daughter's godly character traits were always evident. Her unique personality displayed her love for God as she honored Him in her life.

BONNIE MAE LIVED UP TO HER NAME

As her parents, we wanted Bonnie Mae to pursue God. Many people are physically beautiful, but their inner character is ungodly. We were pleased how Bonnie developed a relationship with God, then shared His love with others through her life.

The intention to name her Mae did not come from a desire for Bonnie to be wealthy, powerful, or someone who controlled others. Karen and I hoped our daughter would serve God.

We watched Bonnie's character develop as she rose above temporal disappointments. She did not seek what most people consider important such as fame, beauty, glamour, or popularity. As Proverbs 31:30 says, "Charm is deceitful, and beauty is vain, but a woman who fears the LORD is to be praised."

Bonnie's greatness came in the form of compassion, humility, and kindness. This is not a natural gift, but a supernatural work of God in those who trust in Him.

THE TRANSFORMATION

Bonnie's journey of faith began when she was seven years old. Up to the time when she made her decision, neither Karen nor I pressured our daughter about her need to follow Jesus.

We learned about Bonnie's decision to make Jesus Christ her Savior and Lord in our car. I will never forget how my daughter, who still needed a booster seat to keep her properly protected as we traveled asked, "Do you know what I just did?"

We said, "No, what did you do?"

"I just asked Jesus into my heart."

Karen and I looked at one another with great surprise. We were inspired by her important decision.

We then talked about what her decisive announcement meant. As her parents we were very happy our daughter, who still a child, wanted God to control her life.

A few days later, I remembered how the apostle Paul wrote a letter to a young man named Timothy. Paul encouraged him to think about how his godly role models lived for Jesus. His grandmother Lois, and mother Eunice, provided Timothy with good examples for him to follow.

From Bonnie's infancy, we prayed she would live her life for Jesus. Karen and I daily instructed her about the importance of a close relationship with God.

Jesus said in Matthew 19:14, "Let the little children come to me and do not hinder them, for to such belongs the kingdom of heaven." God wants young children to place their faith in

His Son Jesus Christ. I always wanted Bonnie to have faith in God. I wanted her to believe He helps, guides, strengthens and comforts those who trust Him.

We appreciate how God communicates with children. They are spiritually sensitive to God's voice. Sadly, His voice becomes harder to hear as children live by the world's standards. Many people think the Bible is outdated and irrelevant, but God's Word foretold this would happen.

Second Peter 3:3-4 says, "knowing this first of all, that scoffers will come in the last days with scoffing, following their own sinful desires. They will say, 'Where is the promise of his coming? For ever since the fathers fell asleep, all things are continuing as they were from the beginning of creation.'" People today continue to deny God and neglect His Word.

As Bonnie's parents, we are grateful for the many friends who showed God's love to our daughter. She knew right from wrong through the love, care, and concern shown by those who followed God.

Christ Jesus has always been faithful to get me through hard times. He empowers me through His Spirit who He placed in my life. I am grateful for what God has enabled me to do as I live for Him.

I take no credit for my achievements. It is God who has worked through my life. I am grateful for God's faithfulness to look beyond my faults and weaknesses. He works in unexpected ways through His undeserved kindness.

To live as God's child does not mean I always get what I ask. Even when I do not receive my request, He is faithful to show me His love and undeserved kindness.

My daughter began her new life in Christ in first grade. I assured her there is never a time when a person is too young, or too old to receive Him. God welcomes and receives everyone who trusts in Him.

Second Corinthians 5:17 summarizes Christ's transformation of those who trust in Him. "Therefore, if anyone is in Christ, he is a new creation. The old has passed away; behold, the new has come."

Jesus Christ has supernaturally exchanged my self-centered focus to give me a new, fresh perspective. Jesus gives me hope and a clear purpose in life.

Troublesome situations do provoke fear and despair. At those times, I look to Jesus. He protects and helps me through my trials. He understands my selfish desires and limited insight. Even when I do not recognize His purpose in my circumstances, I rely upon Him to get me through my hardships.

CHILDLIKE FAITH

I relate to King David who expressed frustration in Psalm 69:2. He said, "I sink in deep mire, where there is no foothold; I have come into deep waters, and the flood sweeps over me."

When I fail to understand what God wants me to do, I trust Him to show me. When I do so, He guides me.

As Jesus said in Matthew 7:7-8, "Ask, and it will be given to you; seek, and you will find; knock, and it will be opened to you. For everyone who asks receives, and the one who seeks finds, and to the one who knocks it will be opened."

Faith is an act of genuine and intentional dependence upon God. Children expect their parents to provide for their needs. In a similar manner, God provides me His help when I seek Him.

Jesus said in Matthew 18:3, "Truly, I say to you, unless you turn and become like children, you will never enter the kingdom of heaven." Such behavior is not childish, immature, or naïve. Faith requires courage, and commitment to God who makes His steadfast presence known to me.

Throughout my childhood, I heard about God, but never gave Him full control of my life. I went to church, but never knew Jesus in an intimate and personal way. The day I repented, and welcomed Jesus into my life, a dramatic change happened in me. I knew He transformed my life in unexpected ways.

No longer do I feel like a caterpillar who needs to crawl through dirty rubbish. Christ's love picks me up every day. He enables me to rise above my circumstances to have a better outlook on life.

When I gave my life to Christ, He took a heavy burden from me. I felt different. My feet were no longer planted in the ground of despair. Jesus took me out of my helpless state.

I have been born again. Jesus gives a new life to all who trust Him. Galatians 2:20 says, "I have been crucified with Christ. It is no longer I who live, but Christ who lives in me. And the life I now live in the flesh I live by faith in the Son of God, who loved me and gave himself for me."

Former oppressive burdens of failure, disappointment, and despair no longer trouble me. Jesus liberated me to live free of my unpleasant memories. He took my life from spiritual darkness into His glorious light. Psalm 103:12 reminds me, "As far as the east is from the west, so far does he remove our transgressions from us."

My shameful thoughts, actions, and outlook no longer control me. As I live for Jesus, He reveals His desire and purpose for me.

My helper, the Holy Spirit, is alive in me. He reminds me of what God wants me to do. Even when I do not always know the purpose of my misfortunes, such as my daughter's death, I trust God to make use of my afflictions for His glory.

When I am weak and unable to go on, Jesus shows me His greatness. Evil powers constantly try to drag me down into despair. Thankfully, the Holy Spirit reminds me of my dependence upon Christ.

Psalm 41:2 says, "the LORD protects him and keeps him alive; he is called blessed in the land; you do not give him up to the will of his enemies." God protects and keeps me from the spiritual forces who are against me as a follower of Jesus Christ.

Hardships draw me closer to God. When I set aside my pride and self-centeredness, God reveals Himself to me. As He empowers me in wearisome times, I trust Him with all my heart. Second Corinthians 12:9b says, "I will boast all the more gladly of my weaknesses, so that the power of Christ may rest upon me."

MY GREATEST LOVE

The evening before my daughter died, Karen's sister stayed overnight with Bonnie in the hospital. She did this so Karen, and I could get some needed rest.

When Karen's sister walked into the room Bonnie said, "I am not giving up." Bonnie spoke with a clear voice, even though her condition had become very weak and fragile.

I believed God would restore my only child to full health, even though she seemed to be at the brink of death. Bonnie's spirit remained strong. I remembered many people in Africa who were in a similar condition. Jesus miraculously healed those who seemed hopelessly beyond repair.

Before I departed Bonnie's room that night, God motivated me to take my daughter's hand. I said to her, "Bonnie, if you hear the voice of Jesus calling you to Himself, follow Jesus. Always follow Jesus."

Never did I think at the time, those would be the last words she would hear me say. Ten hours later, she died. Before I left Bonnie that night, I surrendered my most valuable treasure to Jesus.

Several times afterward I thought, "Did I give up on her too soon?" Every time the troublesome condemnation came to my mind, God graciously assured me that I never gave up on my daughter.

Psalm 139:16 assures me God knew how long Bonnie would live before she was born. Acts 17:24-28 also reminds me God places everyone on earth at the time and place He decided from the beginning of creation.

God awakened me to the fact there is much more to life than what I experience here on earth. An eternal life awaits all who live for Christ.

God comforts me in my loss. Scripture assures me Bonnie has gone on in her life journey. I, too, will be reunited with her in the near future. To never say goodbye again shall be an extraordinary experience.

LISTEN TO GOD'S VOICE

I encouraged Bonnie to "listen to the voice of Jesus." Those whose hearts and minds are focused on Him can know God's desire for them.

God spoke with people in clear and direct ways throughout the Bible. He also communicates with me so I can learn from Him. As a follower of Jesus, God gives me His Spirit who helps me to know and accomplish His desires in me. John 14:16-17 refers to the Holy Spirit as a helper, teacher, and comforter.

Before I accepted Christ as my Savior, I lived as an unrepentant and rebellious person. I did not know God nor His Holy Spirit. After I received Jesus Christ as my Savior, I developed a close relationship with Him. My life continues to change as He transforms my life through the Holy Spirit.

Many times, I do not receive a clear response from God. I get confused and uncertain about what to do. When such times occur, I pray. God will show me His desire. As Jeremiah 33:3 says, "Call to me and I will answer you, and will tell you great and hidden things that you have not known."

God restores my soul. He gives me comfort and hope about my future. I trust Him even when I cannot hear His voice or recognize His plan.

I am grateful eternal life is part of Christ's salvation. He empowers me to turn from earthly passions, as the Holy Spirit encourages me to follow God's Word wholeheartedly.

Ephesians 1:7-9 reminds me, "In him we have redemption through his blood, the forgiveness of our trespasses, according to the riches of his grace, which he lavished upon us, in all wisdom and insight making known to us the mystery of his will, which he set forth in Christ."

NO BLAME

Daily I trust God to uphold and strengthen me as I deeply miss Bonnie. She understood me like no one else. We interacted with each other in a unique way.

After decades of marriage, my wife and I still frequently misunderstand one another. However, Bonnie could recognize, interpret, and explain my intentions to Karen. She helped my communication skills and provided harmony in our home.

When such a person goes away, they are greatly missed. Disappointments arise as many of my unkind responses are left unaddressed. Bonnie's ability to offer feedback about my behavior in a positive way helped both Karen and I tremendously.

Today I pray about areas where my behavior needs to change. As I study Scripture, I ask God to give me insight from His Word. God then graciously reveals to me what I need to do.

John 9:1-41 talks about what happened when Jesus healed a blind man. Religious leaders did not like how Jesus restored the man's vision on a Sabbath day. They were more upset about a broken rule rather than appreciating the transformation done in the man's life.

I found myself much like the religious leaders. I had expectations of what God should have done, then failed to recognize His mercy in the situation.

When Bonnie died, she experienced a great change. She is now in heaven where there is no more pain, sickness, or suffering. Her condition instantly changed, as did the blind man's situation when he received his sight.

I still wrestle with the death of my daughter, but God graciously reminds me of my responsibility and purpose in life. I can stay angry at Him and myself about Bonnie's death, or I can refocus on my privilege to live each day for Him.

I also learned from the account in Luke 15:11-32. I must choose to get out of my emotional pig pen and turn back to God. He does not want me to live in my hopeless condition. God knows I hurt. He is faithful to help me out of my misery.

Through God's Son, Jesus Christ, I have been made new. His glorious transformation is far greater than anything this world offers me. Jesus Christ daily gives me the ability to overcome my hardships.

I no longer ask God why terrible and painful trials happen. Instead, I trust God who knows about the troublesome situation, and who makes miracles happen. This is why I pray for everyone who needs His assistance, and humbly request Him to provide for them.

Leviticus 16 refers to a scapegoat who symbolically took

blame upon itself. Christ already has taken my heavy burdens so He can comfort me and others who are afflicted.

Jesus understands my intense pain. Matthew 26:39 reminds me how Jesus cried out, "My Father, if it be possible, let this cup pass from me; nevertheless, not as I will, but as you will."

As I place my trust in Christ, He protects me against the harassment of Satan. Jesus empowers me to remain steadfast in my relationship with Him.

A RIVER TO CROSS

Two hymns that provided me great comfort after Bonnie's death are "I Will Sing the Wondrous Story" by Francis Rowley, and "It is Well with My Soul" by Horatio Spafford.

Both songs were written in the 1800s. At that time, a river implied physical death and a place beyond this world. These ideas developed through Scripture references about a river. Isaiah 66:12 likens a river to a refreshing stream, and John 7:38 alludes to a river as an abundant fulfillment given to those who believe in Jesus Christ.

"It is Well with My Soul" describes a river as peace in the certainty of death. Rowley, on the other hand, reflects upon a river as the eternal satisfaction Christ gives His believers.

Rowley and Spafford both proclaimed how Jesus welcomes His followers to heaven when they die. Jesus promised to give eternal life to all who believe in Him as their Savior (John 3:16).

These songs reflect upon the fact Jesus died on the cross. Through Christ's sacrifice, I am free to live a new life. I am empowered by the Holy Spirit to honor God as I live for Him.

When Bonnie died, my emotions overwhelmed me. Just as a turbulent river removes everything in its path, the powerful force of death took my sight off of God's goodness. Thankfully by the grace of Christ's salvation, He got me out of my hopeless pit.

The Holy Spirit assures me God is my stronghold. As Psalm 56:13 says, "For you have delivered my soul from death, yes, my feet from falling." The life I have in Christ gives me peace as He renews my life each day.

The gift of eternal life through Christ's death and resurrection has released me from my desire to always be in control. Daily I seek His help in hardships, and trust in His intervention. With God I do not fear the river of death, for He is with me wherever I go.

Instead, I love to sing of His wondrous work in me. I am eternally grateful how Jesus placed the Holy Spirit in me. Through Him I have been able to honestly confront my doubts, fears, and internal conflicts.

I deeply miss my daughter who left this life and is now with God in heaven. Thankfully, I am comforted by Christ as He assures me about great things yet to come.

AN INTERNAL BATTLE

Jesus is patient, and wants me to trust Him, even after my great loss. His provisions of love and forgiveness assure me of my future. Not even death is able to separate me from God.

No matter how turbulent my life becomes, Jesus is vigilant and merciful. He has my best interest in mind. His delays and denials are ways He gets my attention. Out of His great love for me He develops my character and faith in Him.

My heart broke as I watched my only child die. My hopes and expectations were shattered. Yet death deepened my relationship with God. My thoughts are much like Paul's in Romans 9:1-2, "I am speaking the truth in Christ – I am not lying; my conscience bears me witness in the Holy Spirit – that I have great and unceasing anguish in my heart."

After her death I regretted what could have, should have, or would have happened if we had had more time together. I also recognized how irritable, sarcastic, and selfish I had become because of my inner frustration and disappointment.

Until I intentionally embraced Christ's love, forgiveness, and empowerment, my bad behavior kept me captive. My regretful actions from the past created an inner battle in my soul. Thankfully Jesus conquered my old nature through His love, mercy, and grace.

The Holy Spirit enables me to be honest with myself. I am aware of my inability to erase hurtful memories. My stubborn self-reliant attitude and actions often hinder me.

Thankfully God makes the most of my painful failures. My restricted outlook reminds me to remember His faithfulness, not my faults. I daily rely upon the Holy Spirit to control my thoughts and behavior.

First Corinthians 13: 9 -13 teaches that I have a limited perspective. This motivates me to intentionally give Jesus my burdens and fears. As I do, He accepts me just as I am, then renews my outlook.

I do not need to "get my act together" before He helps me. Christ's forgiveness empowers me to forgive myself. My inner battle is defeated when I focus my thoughts on Christ.

MY DAILY ROUTINES

Since May 1978, I have enjoyed and appreciated my bond with Christ. My relationship with Him has grown as I study the Holy Bible and pray. My connection with Christ involves an engaged and honest conversation with Him. I come to Jesus as my Lord. He is a friend who cares for me.

As a dedicated follower of Jesus, I still get distracted and take my focus off Him. When this happens, He can seem to be far away from me. Thankfully Jesus never leaves me, and even when I depart from Him, He keeps watch over me.

The acrostic ACTS help to guide my thoughts as I pray. First, I always "Acknowledge" God's greatness and power over me. There is no authority greater than God Himself. He is trustworthy.

After I acknowledge God's goodness and righteousness, I humbly "Confess" my unworthiness to receive His undeserved kindness. I do not demand God's approval but request His help.

As a believer of Jesus Christ, I do my best to live for Him. Nonetheless, my old nature still causes me to resist God's desire for me. When I confess to God my inability to live as I should, Jesus assures me of His love.

God has adopted me as His child. He has taken away my faults and shortcomings. My heavenly Father always receives and accepts me as His treasured possession. Even though I am weak and fail Him, He never abandons me.

With this in mind, I "Thank" God for His unconditional acceptance of me. I am aware of my daily need for His help and trust Him to provide for me. As I do so, His Holy Spirit reveals God's blessings in my life.

Then I give my "Supplications" or requests to God. I speak to Him honestly as my friend and Savior who loves me. My supplications also include the needs of others when I ask Him to help those who suffer.

When I pray, I want to know Him better. A mutual relationship requires meaningful communication between two individuals. I have learned to discern God's desire for me as I pray. Then through insights found in Scripture, He guides me to respond in a proper manner through my trials.

Repentance requires me to turn from my self-centered ways and trust Him. Sometimes the requests I pray for are not answered in the way I hope. I then have a choice to seek His counsel or proceed without Him.

My desire is to trust God through my difficult circumstances. As 1 Peter 5:10 says, "And after you have suffered a little while, the God of all grace, who has called you to his eternal glory in Christ, will himself restore, confirm, strengthen, and establish you."

Daily I experience Christ's empowerment as I seek Him above my own desires. He is faithful to reveal Himself to me in unexpected ways as I love, obey, and honor Him.

God graciously guides me through difficult situations. I experience His presence with me. He never abandons me in my distress. This is why I trust Him to help me through each and every day.

HELPFUL PROMISES AND ENCOURAGEMENT ABOUT GOD'S INVITATION TO OBEY HIM

"If my people who are called by my name humble themselves, and pray and seek my face and turn from their wicked ways, then I will hear from heaven and will forgive their sin and heal their land" 2 Chronicles 7:14.

"I love the LORD, because he has heard my voice and my pleas for mercy. Because he inclined his ear to me, therefore I will call on him as long as I live" Psalm 116:1-2.

"Seek the LORD while he may be found; call upon him while he is near; let the wicked forsake his way, and the unrighteous man his thoughts; let him return to the LORD, that he may have compassion on him, and to our God, for he will abundantly pardon" Isaiah 55:6-7.

"The Lord is good to those who wait for him, to the soul who seeks him" Lamentations 3:25.

"For everyone who exalts himself will be humbled, and he who humbles himself will be exalted" Luke 14:11.

"Jesus answered him, 'Truly, truly, I say to you, unless one is born again he cannot see the kingdom of God'" John 3:3.

"May the God of hope fill you with all joy and peace in believing, so that by the power of the Holy Spirit you may abound in hope" Romans 15:13.

"For we are glad when we are weak and you are strong. Your restoration is what we pray for" 2 Corinthians 13:9.

"Since then we have a great high priest who has passed through the heavens, Jesus, the Son of God, let us hold fast to our confession. For we do not have a high priest who is unable to sympathize with our weaknesses, but one who in every respect has been tempted as we are, yet without sin" Hebrews 4:14-15.

CHAPTER 9
HEAVEN

"Set your minds on things that are above, not on things that are
on earth. For you have died, and your life is hidden with Christ
in God. When Christ who is your life appears, then you also
will appear with him in glory"
Colossians 3:2-4.

Bonnie and I trusted Jesus Christ to heal her cancer. My wife
Karen had a different perspective. She always believed our
daughter's ultimate restoration would take place in heaven.

Years after Bonnie's death, I struggled to embrace Karen's
conviction. My loss overshadowed the great and extraordinary
transition my daughter experienced. I know in my head
Bonnie's life is now far better off, but my heart still misses her
very much.

The Bible refers to the heart in a symbolic way. My human
heart performs an essential physical function in me. Without a
healthy heart my body and mind will not function properly.
Scripture also relates the heart to the place where influential
thoughts and emotions dwell.

Proverbs 16:9 says, "The heart of a man plans his way, but the LORD establishes his steps." King David also said in 1 Chronicles 28:9, "And you, Solomon my son, know the God of your father and serve him with a whole heart and with a willing mind, for the Lord searches all hearts and understands every plan and thought. If you seek him, he will be found by you, but if you forsake him, he will cast you off forever."

Bonnie impacted me beyond measure. Her departure created a huge void in my life. An important person in my life is no longer here to give me encouragement. My daughter expressed love and appreciation which provided me great insights throughout the brief time we enjoyed together here on earth.

The immense emotional pain of sadness and sorrow burdened me. Nevertheless, I now understand better how a major physical or emotional wound does not heal quickly.

Through my struggle I have managed to acquire comfort and relief about my daughter's physical absence. As I trust Jesus to restore my broken heart, He has given me realistic expectations of the eternal home He has prepared for me.

Bonnie's death "took the wind out of my sails." I do not have the energy and drive to complete projects the way I used to.

I have come to realize things do not always turn out the way I expect. Therefore, I now seek to manage my time better so I can accomplish what God wants me to do.

I daily give my cares and concerns to God. He in return is faithful to provide wisdom, and contentment in the fact this world is only temporary. Isaiah 40:8 says, "The grass withers, the flower fades, but the word of our God will stand forever."

When I focus my attention on things above, the things of earth lose their enticement. God enables me to be content with my life. I have satisfaction in the fact that my joy does not come from this world. My joy comes from God. God's desire is for me to be thankful for His help in my life as I trust Him.

When life makes no sense at all, I look up, and trust God to reveal Himself. My heart's desire is to obey Him, especially when circumstances cause me to question His plan for my life.

MISERY BEFORE RELIEF

As an active-duty airman in the United States Air Force, my final assignment took me to Missouri, which is known as the "Show Me" state.

I experienced extreme cold in the winter months, and intense summer heat in Missouri. When I spoke to native residents about their weather conditions they jokingly replied, "It's okay, it's just misery."

Their good-natured response reflected a "show me" attitude. They accepted the weather they had and added some humor to maintain a positive outlook. There is indeed misery before relief arrives.

I live in this world full of disappointment, misery, and despair. However, there is Good News. Jesus saves all who believe in Him!

As my Savior, Jesus gives me hope as He influences my life. Psalm 146:8 describes several accomplishments He has done for me, "the LORD opens the eyes of the blind, the LORD lifts up those who are bowed down; the LORD loves the righteous." I am grateful for His undeserved kindness.

Jesus lifted me out of my spiritual darkness so I could experience spiritual enlightenment. He guides me as I trust Him through my troublesome circumstances. His forgiveness has made me right with God.

I am weak and imperfect. I am unable to remove the pain I suffer because of this fallen world. Nonetheless, when Jesus died on the cross, He took the curse of sin upon Himself. He liberated me from the bondage that sin once had upon my life.

Instead of death, Jesus has given me eternal life. He has made known God's purpose in this spiritually darkened world. John 8:12 points out, "Jesus spoke to them, saying, I am the light of the world. Whoever follows me will not walk in darkness but will have the light of life." Christ's salvation and deliverance have changed me.

I am grateful Jesus has worked far beyond my own expectations. He gives me faith, and perseverance to get through my hardships every day.

THE VEIL IS LIFTED

Hope is the conviction, along with a confident trust, that circumstances will change. The current condition of our miserable world is obvious. Thankfully, change happens as God intervenes on behalf of His people.

I experienced this truth when I went along with a group of friends to the Sears Tower in Chicago. We wanted to see the lights of the city from the top of that building. When we reached the observation deck, on the top floor, nothing but a thick fog could be seen.

Most of the group saw the dark cloud, then quickly returned to the van. A few of us stayed behind to pray. We asked God to lift the fog, and within moments, the thick fog vanished. The sight seemed unreal as the city lights became visible. It seemed impossible for such a dramatic change to happen so quickly. We stared in awe at the sight for quite some time.

Eventually we returned to the bus. Those who left early asked, "What took you so long?" Most were in stunned disbelief when they heard how God had removed the dense fog, and we enjoyed an incredible view.

Through this experience, I learned the importance of hope in an unlikely situation. When I trust God to do a miracle, wonderful changes can happen. "For he satisfies the longing soul, and the hungry soul he fills with good things" (Psalm 107:9).

As Jesus taught God's Word He restored and transformed the lives of many who believed in Him. Other people saw Jesus do great miracles, yet they refused to accept or believe in Him. Sadly, most people today still reject Jesus in a similar way.

Jesus warned about the result of unbelief in John 12:47-48; "If anyone hears my words and does not keep them, I do not judge him; for I did not come to judge the world but to save the world. The one who rejects me and does not receive my words has a judge; the word that I have spoken will judge him on the last day."

Everyone who accepts Christ's Good News is promised eternal life. For those who reject Him, their unbelief shall judge them. On God's judgment day unbelievers will suffer an eternity of endless misery.

A common question I hear from unbelievers is, "What happens to those who never hear about Christ's Good News?" Romans 1:19-20 says God has already made Himself known to them through His creation. Everyone has an awareness of God and knows their need of Him. No one is without excuse for their sinful behavior.

Jesus Christ wants to rescue everyone from certain destruction and death. I am grateful how He has kept watch over my life here on earth. He has also promised to receive me into heaven when I die.

I live in a world full of misery and despair. Thankfully Jesus Christ has saved and restored me! He has taken my bad and unacceptable behavior and made me right with God. Jesus took me out of spiritual darkness into His glorious light. My life has been drastically changed.

I am grateful how God goes beyond expectations. As I trust Him, He surpasses my wildest dreams. He replaces my dark veil of despair with the promise of better days to come.

MY MOMENTARY CONDITION

Second Corinthians 5:1 compares my physical existence to a tent. My physical form identifies me as a person who is different from everyone else.

Over time my human frame becomes weak because of the continual wear and tear upon it. Sometimes parts of my body get damaged. As I age, I become weaker and lose strength.

My human body is very complex. It can often repair itself after an injury. Unfortunately, old age can weaken parts of my body to the point that they become permanently irreparable.

When God spoke our universe into existence, His creation developed exactly as He planned. According to Ecclesiastes 3:11, God put in our hearts a knowledge that life does not end at death.

The Holy Bible teaches me how God desires me to have a meaningful relationship with Him. He gives everybody free will to follow Him or reject Him. Unfortunately, most people choose to disobey God's true Word.

My decision to follow God has an eternal impact upon me. Hebrews 9:27-28 warns that all people are given one life to live, and then comes their judgment. There is no second chance for anyone to receive His salvation after they die.

This is why I have committed myself to love and obey Christ. When Jesus died on the cross for my sins, He made it possible for me to have a personal relationship with God.

Both unbelievers and Christ followers die on earth. At death a person has the appearance of someone who has fallen asleep. However, they cannot wake up because their soul has left their physical body.

I determine whether my eternal destination will be in heaven or in hell. My acceptance of Christ's sacrifice on my behalf gives me eternal life with Him. If I reject Christ, I will spend eternity separated from God.

I am excited about what God has in store for me after I take my last breath here on earth. I have no fear of death because God promises me an eternal home with Him made possible through His Son Jesus Christ.

MY IMPERISHABLE SOUL

I gained much insight through the completion of my three post graduate degrees. Two are in the field of theology, the other is in counseling.

I do not claim to be an expert in the field of counseling, but my passion to acquire greater insight from the Holy Bible is a daily quest. Both counseling and Scripture provide insight into what motivates the actions of people.

Every individual has a unique identity, this is defined by the word psyche, or what is known as the human soul. Just as God created everyone with unique fingerprints, He also made each soul unique. My soul reveals who I am as a human being.

Psalm 139:6 says, "Such knowledge is too wonderful for me; it is high; I cannot attain it." To fully understand a person's psyche is impossible, but the soul of an individual can be known by their unique characteristics.

A soul is not physical matter, nor is it a misty looking spirit. A person's soul is an eternal representation of one's life. The physical body dies, but the soul never decays or decomposes.

When an individual dies, the soul leaves their physical body. God carefully receives every soul to Himself as they await their final destination, heaven or hell.

Fortunately, the Bible gives insight into how people are known and identified by others. One reference in 1 Samuel 28:12-15 details how the witch of Endor brought up a spirit for King Saul.

When King Saul spoke with the departed soul of Samuel, he did so through the assistance of a medium who communicated with the dead. People who do this get insight from evil spirits who do not represent God.

Psalm 96:4-5 clearly says, "For great is the LORD, and greatly to be praised, he is to be feared above all gods. For all the gods of the peoples are worthless idols." This is why the first of the Ten Commandments says, "You shall have no other gods before me" (Exodus 20:3).

God's Word strictly warns people never to contact a person's soul after they die. These warnings are found in Leviticus 19:31; 20:6, 27 and Deuteronomy 18:10-12. Those who communicate with the dead are influenced by demonic forces who deceive them.

If a person seeks a supernatural power other than God's Son, Jesus Christ, they are at risk of losing their own soul. Just as Saul who once knew God died a miserable death without Him.

THERE IS LIFE AFTER DEATH

The New Testament gives three examples where souls were seen after their physical death. Moses and Elijah both met with Jesus on the Mount of Transfiguration in Matthew 17:1-8. Another passage notes Lazarus communicated with a rich man after he died in Luke 16:19-31.

Both accounts seem to reveal departed souls are very much alive.

Hebrews 12:1 also mentions a great cloud of witnesses that are seen in heaven. This cloud does not refer to a large water vapor in the sky, but rather a very large group of people who died as Christ's followers. They are gathered in a place God prepared for those who love Him.

Some say these events were a vision. Nevertheless, in each instance the people who died were recognized by others. These reports recorded in the Holy Bible give evidence to the fact that a human soul is immortal.

I am comforted to know my loved ones are clearly seen and recognized as people who once lived on earth. I eagerly wait for the time when God will call me home to heaven.

THE METAPHYSICAL

The human body has many unseen parts which have an important function. Lungs take in invisible oxygen. Then the oxygen is circulated throughout a person's body through their blood. This is necessary for the health of all living beings.

The human soul is invisible, but it provides a very real and essential role in every person. Every soul can be known and appreciated for their unique part in God's creation.

A good modern representation of the metaphysical dimension is found in the Marvel movie, *Doctor Strange*. This motion picture gives insight into the metaphysical dimension. It reveals how God's creation can be manipulated by spiritual forces. These forces can be evil and demonic.

Several characters in the movie lose their humanness as they pursue control and power which destroys their souls. Aspirations influenced by demonic practices put these individuals into a dark, hopeless, and miserable condition.

King Solomon wrote in Ecclesiastes 2:26 how those who live to honor God gain His wisdom, knowledge, and joy. However, those who pursue their own selfish desires find themselves unsatisfied and discontented.

Jesus makes a similar observation in Matthew 16:26, "For what will it profit a man if he gains the whole world and forfeits his soul? Or what shall a man give in return for his soul?"

I am mindful of God's judgment yet to come. The supernatural realm is not mine to fully understand. Yet it is real, and everyone needs Christ's protection from evil forces.

This is why Ephesians 6:10-17 encourages believers to protect themselves from evil, supernatural powers that are at war with God. This spiritual battle against ungodly forces is only overcome through the spiritual armor given by God.

From the moment I decided to follow Jesus Christ in my life, I recognized my inability to fight spiritual battles through my own strength or understanding. I have no need or desire to struggle with the devil.

Jesus Christ has saved and restored my life here on earth. He promises me an eternal life with Him in heaven because I trust Him. Daily Jesus gives me needed confidence and strength to endure my struggles.

I have no fear of death. Instead, I trust Jesus. As He says in Matthew 10:28, "Do not fear those who kill the body but cannot kill the soul. Rather fear him who can destroy both soul and body in hell."

THE HOPE OF HEAVEN

A few days before my only child died, her cancer doctor informed me about Bonnie's likely death. She highly recommended Bonnie's endorsement of a Do Not Resuscitate order (DNR).

As her parents, neither Karen nor I could make the important decision for Bonnie. She was over eighteen years of age and had to sign the papers herself. My task was to convince Bonnie to sign the DNR order.

Bonnie's physically weak body probably would not have survived the traumatic attempts needed to revive her heart. My daughter's vocal cords were badly damaged from the photon radiation, and the brain tumor had paralyzed her from the neck down.

My inability to clearly hear Bonnie speak made it difficult to discuss this with her. I needed sensitive discernment as I approached my daughter about signing the DNR papers. My heart broke to see my daughter in such a weak condition, but I held on to my faith in God's awesome grace.

Bonnie and I confidently trusted God to overcome her cancer. I knew the task assigned to me would be very difficult. Like my daughter, I also believed God would do a miracle and heal her.

I did not like the fact that no effort would be made to revive her. Never did Bonnie or I give up hope in God's ability to heal her. We both knew He could do a supernatural restoration in her. Even when life appears to be lost and hopeless, He can renew those who trust Him.

This is why Jesus said in Matthew 5:12, "Rejoice and be glad, for your reward is great in heaven." Christ can restore and empower those who trust Him. Nonetheless, everyone's physical life, both young and old, will come to an end on earth someday. As a believer of Jesus, I am comforted to know God will receive me into heaven when I die.

First Corinthians 13:12 also says, "For now we see in a mirror dimly, but then face to face. Now I know in part; then I should know fully, even as I have been fully known." My understanding of heaven here on earth is limited. Heaven is far greater than anyone can imagine.

While here on earth I struggle to understand God's plans. I know only a small part of His big picture. Nonetheless, I daily seek to know Him better. I have learned to trust God for needed insight to help me through my life, especially in difficult circumstances.

DISCERNMENT GIVEN BY GOD

Bonnie needed to sign the DNR order because of her weak and declining condition. Death seemed inevitable, but this did not shake my daughter's belief in God's power to heal her.

I told her if medical personnel were able to restart her heart, a ventilator would be needed to artificially keep her alive. However, this did not convince Bonnie to accept the DNR order.

At the beginning of her life, only a few weeks after birth, she went through a serious physical setback. Yet, God restored her after that near death experience. I detected Bonnie's facial expression of confusion and disappointment as I encouraged her to sign the papers. She showed no interest in signing them since she expected to overcome her cancer.

I then silently asked God to reveal what the Holy Bible said to help me deal with my dilemma. He reminded me of Psalm 90:10. This verse tells the likelihood of a person to live to seventy, or maybe eighty years of age, if they are really strong.

Moses wrote this more than 3,000 years ago, and it is still true today. Even with the many modern medical breakthroughs, life expectancy still ranges from seventy to eighty years of age.

Psalm 90:10 also mentions how at death, God receives

people to Himself. The last breath taken on earth begins a new adventure for Christ's believers in heaven.

The Holy Spirit also reminds me how James 4:14 compares life on earth to a fine mist or vapor. Even if I am able to live seventy or eighty years in my earthly body, in comparison to eternity, my brief time here on earth is much like a morning fog. After a warm sunrise the water vapor quickly vanishes away. I told Bonnie it would only be a few more years until I joined her in heaven.

As I reflected on these biblical thoughts about the brevity of life on earth, and the promise of heaven, I saw an immediate change in Bonnie's countenance. Moments earlier her eyes reflected shock and despair about our conversation, but then she brightened up.

Darkness turned into light as the hope of God's Word provided comfort to her weary soul. There is much more to life than what is experienced on earth.

She whispered, "Okay Daddy, if you will be in heaven with me soon, I will sign the DNR papers." Because of Bonnie's weakness and paralysis, Karen needed to hold her hand up as she signed the forms.

The reality and assurance of God's salvation provided by her Savior Jesus Christ, allowed Bonnie to joyfully accept His promise of eternal life. There is no need to fear death for those who are in Christ.

Romans 8:11 says, "If the Spirit of him who raised Jesus from the dead dwells in you, he who raised Christ Jesus from the dead will also give life to your mortal bodies through his Spirit who dwells in you." God's Spirit and eternal life are given to everyone who puts their faith in Jesus Christ.

My faith is in what I hope for but is not yet seen. I am grateful for Christ who made it possible to live with Him in heaven. Yet, as I await heaven, I trust Him to use me for His honor and glory here on earth.

After Christ's death and resurrection Jesus spoke to Thomas who doubted Him. "Jesus said to him, 'Have you believed because you have seen me? Blessed are those who have not seen and yet have believed'" (John 20:29). I have never physically seen Jesus, but I have chosen to live for Him. As I do so, He empowers me through His Holy Spirit.

MY JOURNEY TO HEAVEN

I enjoy the Adirondack Park in New York State. Several trails provide views of lakes, waterfalls, and the opportunity to see other nearby mountain peaks. As I hike the trails, most of my journeys require strong shoes to grab the steep path on the mountain covered by tall, mature trees.

Tiny colored markers placed on trees along a trail can be easily missed. If a person hikes alone and gets lost on one of the many remote trails, serious consequences can unexpectedly happen.

A friend had such an experience. On an unfamiliar, isolated trail she accidentally went off course. She spent several days alone on the mountain. Years later I continue to pray for her recovery from her emotional trauma and physical injuries.

I also have been lost and alone on a path that was difficult to navigate. I am aware that loneliness and weakness do not help me get back on course. When I am tempted to take control through my own understanding, life soon gets out of order.

After Bonnie died. I felt alone, abandoned, and discouraged. Many people gave me love, and encouragement, but my loss kept me depressed and isolated.

When I left my straight and narrow path, darkness overwhelmed me. I needed to intentionally look up, and trust God with every ounce of my strength. As I have done so He has been faithful to lift me up.

Through the help of the Holy Spirit, I have been given strength and guidance to get through my emotionally dark days. As I keep my relationship in tune with God, He helps me experience His goodness.

Some people say my faith in Christ is a crutch. In many ways that is true. As I lean upon God, He always gives me His comfort and strength in my weakness. I am totally dependent upon God to help me change my self-focused outlook that causes me harm.

As 1 John 1:8-9 says, "If we say we have no sin, we deceive ourselves, and the truth is not in us. If we confess our sins, he is faithful and just to forgive us our sins and to cleanse us from all unrighteousness."

I am extremely grateful for God's Son, Jesus Christ. He lived a sinless life, died on the cross, then rose to life to set me free from my sinful condition. As His follower Jesus daily gives me an abundant life with Him.

JOY GIVEN AT THE CROSS

Bonnie, as well as many other children, have expressed sincere thoughts through drawing a picture. Their portraits often showed themselves as a happy stick figure. Often, they placed the cross of Jesus Christ near them.

At an early age, children experience and express their joy in Jesus Christ. His cross serves as a reminder of His great sacrifice, and the need to follow Him.

Jesus, in John 10:28, promises a lifelong relationship with those who trust Him. "I give them eternal life, and they will never perish, and no one will snatch them out of my hand."

Even when I stumble and fall, He picks me up and strengthens me.

Karen and I trust in God's reliable Word. The Holy Bible instructs us about the abundant life God gives to those who pursue and obey Him.

First Thessalonians 4:16-17 speaks of a day to come when my daughter's physical body will be reunited with her eternal soul. In the meantime, I am confident God keeps her, along with all His followers in a glorious place where they live with Him.

Hebrews 11:13-16 also reminds me about how my citizenship is not here on earth. My true home is with God in heaven above. This world is not my permanent home.

In the meantime, I encourage others to follow Jesus. Christ's believers have an incredible journey here on earth, and an awareness that the best is yet to come.

HELPFUL PROMISES AND ENCOURAGEMENT TO REMEMBER THAT HEAVEN IS REAL!

"Enoch walked with God, and he was not, for God took him" Genesis 5:24.

"Elijah went up by a whirlwind into heaven" 2 Kings 2:11.

"The years of their life are seventy, or even by reason of strength eighty; yet their span is but toil and trouble; they are soon gone, and we fly away" Psalm 90:10.

"Jesus said to her, 'I am the resurrection and the life. Whoever believes in me, though he die, yet shall he live, and everyone who lives and believes in me shall never die. Do you believe this?'" John 11:25-26.

"For the Lord himself will descend from heaven with a cry of command, with the voice of an archangel, and with the sound of the trumpet of God. And the dead in Christ will rise first. Then we who are alive, who are left, will be caught up together with them in the clouds to meet the Lord in the air, and so we will always be with the Lord" 1 Thessalonians 4:16-17.

"And just as it is appointed for man to die once, and after that comes judgment, so Christ, having been offered once to bear the sins of many, will appear a second time, not to deal with sin but to save those who are eagerly waiting for him" Hebrews 9:27-28.

"But as it is, they desire a better country, that is, a heavenly one. Therefore, God is not ashamed to be called their God, for he has prepared for them a city" Hebrews 11:16.

"Therefore, since we are surrounded by so great a cloud of witnesses, let us also lay aside every weight, and sin which clings so closely, and let us run with endurance the race that is set before us" Hebrews 12:1.

"Because you have kept my word about patient endurance, I will keep you from the hour of trial that is coming on the whole world, to try those who dwell on the earth. I am coming soon. Hold fast what you have, so that no one may seize your crown" Revelation 3:10-11.

CHAPTER 10
GRIEF

"But we do not want you to be uninformed, brothers, about those who are asleep, that you may not grieve as others who have no hope."
1 Thessalonians 4:13

I mourn the death of my daughter. My fun, insightful and cheerful days with Bonnie are now only treasured memories. Our common interests, outlooks on life, and love for adventure helped us to develop a very close bond with one another. Without Bonnie, my life has not been the same.

There are different ways a person can grieve. Some think the only way to mourn is to shed tears and have emotional outbursts. In biblical days, people were paid to grieve in such a way.

Tears and cries of sorrow are natural ways to grieve. God has placed in every person a natural ability to release emotional sadness in healthy and nondestructive ways.

Some people, like me, do not easily disclose their anguish. I normally do not outwardly display my grief.

I am aware of my need to grieve and release the built-up stress inside of me. When negative emotions are stored internally, pressures in my body and mind increase. Sickness, headaches, injuries, and emotional outbursts are common side effects of accumulated internal stress.

Because of my tendency to control my outward expressions of dissatisfaction, I need to remind myself of the need to release built-up emotions. Stretching exercises, long walks, inhaling deeply and prayer help to ease my pain.

Even though I do not cry a lot, my emotional distress is evident as I mourn. My facial countenance and irritable behavior are noticed by others.

As it is written in Nehemiah 2:2, "And the king said to me, 'Why is your face sad, seeing you are not sick? This is nothing but sadness of the heart.'" Proverbs 13:12 also says, "Hope deferred makes the heart sick, but a desire fulfilled is a tree of life." The condition of my heart is easily seen by others.

Many people use drugs, alcohol, and other methods to hide their pain. When abused and overused their remedies cause more problems.

God's Word encourages me to recognize my grief, give my burdens to Jesus and trust Him to restore me. My loss has helped me to be more aware of others who grieve.

A RENEWED PERSPECTIVE

When I am sad, I intentionally seek God's help. He uses grief to help me understand my need for Him. I recognize the pain my loss has caused me.

The death of my only child has been extremely difficult to understand. Her death caused me to think about what is most important in my life. I realize what I appreciate most here on earth is my close relationship with God.

God provides everything I need here on earth. I am grateful for how He has given me His peace through my hardships, trials, and loss.

After Bonnie's death, Jesus reminded me there is much He wants to show me on earth, and in heaven to come. The reality of heaven gets easily lost when I focus on myself. When earthly pleasures become more important than God, I lose sight of my final destination.

In Matthew 6:22-23 Jesus said, "The eye is the lamp of the body. So, if your eye is healthy, your whole body will be full of light, but if your eye is bad, your whole body will be full of darkness. If then the light in you is darkness, how great is the darkness!"

My inability to comprehend why Bonnie died gave rise to an emotional and spiritual crisis within me. I needed relief from my distress and grief.

Bonnie's death created a huge void in me. The relationship I once enjoyed with my daughter no longer existed.

My displeasure about my situation needed to change. The Holy Spirit reminded me Jesus had restored my broken past, and I needed to trust Him to do it again.

My thoughts reflected Psalm 51:10-12, "Create in me a clean heart, O God, and renew a right spirit within me. Cast me not away from your presence, and take not your Holy Spirit from me. Restore to me the joy of your salvation, and uphold me with a willing spirit."

God brought light into my darkened life. He reminded me of His faithfulness. These memories gave me hope, and a desire to crawl out of the pit I found myself in.

RAISED BY THE GREATEST GENERATION

My life slowed down significantly after Bonnie died. I reflected more upon God and His greatness as I thought about my sorrow. I know about my past and present but am uncertain what will happen in the future. God assured me I have nothing to fear.

My life is much like a parade. There has been a progression of events with a beginning, middle, and an end. I have looked back on my past and seen how God has helped me. I know He is with me now and He knows the end of my life's story. I am grateful how God has helped me to persevere through difficulties.

Throughout my life I have encountered unforeseen obstacles. Adjustments to new environments, communication challenges, and the uncertainty about my future have caused me to be cautious when I make decisions.

My earthly perspective has limits. Nevertheless, I need faith as I hope for a certain outcome. I need to trust God and ask for His help in troublesome situations.

Nahum 1:7 reminds me, "The LORD is good, a stronghold in the day of trouble; he knows those who take refuge in him." God is my trustworthy Savior.

My Australian friends like to tell me, "She'll be right, mate." However, their positive attitude does not always reflect my thoughts. My doubts cause me to lack assurance about the future.

James 1:5-6 motivates me to trust God. "If any of you lacks wisdom, let him ask God, who gives generously to all without reproach, and it will be given him. But let him ask in faith, with no doubting, for the one who doubts is like a wave of the sea that is driven and tossed by the wind."

Thankfully God knows my past and present, as well as my

future. He is above me and wants to influence my plans and actions. When I allow Him to work through me, His light shines in the darkness.

God's Word instructs me to do what is right. My actions have consequences. Therefore, commitment and perseverance are needed to be faithful.

I knew many people from the World War II era who went from poverty to abundance. They overcame great hardships. Biblical values helped guide my parents and most of their generation. This generation knew right from wrong according to the Holy Bible. They made their decisions based on the truth of God's Word.

My parents were far from perfect. However, as a home-maker, my mom always provided me needed comfort and security through her unconditional love. Mom motivated me to develop my own sincere faith in Christ, and she provided me a good example of how to live a godly life.

My father showed little interest in my life and frequently withdrew himself from family activities. Before I was born, my father served as a crew member on a B-17 airplane in World War II.

As a bombardier, on his thirty-one missions, he quickly became an aerial gunner. Immediately after their bombardments, enemy fighters would attack them.

I learned about my dad's missions from his obituary after he died. Books written by former B-17 crew members helped me understand the difficult environment airmen endured in WWII. My father never spoke about his horrific experiences.

My dad received the distinguished Flying Cross, an Air Force Medal with three bronze clusters on it, along with other military awards. Those recognitions of valor serve as a reminder for me to persevere, as well as to be strong and courageous when I am in difficult situations.

When I reflect upon my past, I also think about how Jesus transformed me. I am grateful Jesus has comforted me regarding my past disappointments. My life is not flawless, yet Jesus enables me to move on from my former failures and leave them with Him.

The Holy Spirit has firmly established a secure foundation in my life. When grief floods my soul with sorrow, I am not enslaved by my troubled emotions. Instead, God's strength, wisdom, and faithfulness carry me through my trials.

DEPENDABLE ADVICE

A very special memento from my father is a silk scarf he wore on his B-17 missions. It has a map of North Africa with Morocco, Algeria, Tunisia, and Libya on one side. On the back is a map of Spain. He wore the scarf to provide directions if his B-17 airplane went down in enemy territory.

A map provides directions in an unfamiliar place. Frequently, I find myself lost, and in need of guidance. This happens when I am tempted to compromise my devotion to God.

My daily study of the Holy Bible is extremely important to me. Usually what I read in the morning, is what God wants me to put into action a few hours later.

When I take the time to study my Bible, I am challenged to look beyond my own concerns. I am more likely to respond to the needs of others when motivated by God's Word. Sometimes I can help and at other times all I can do is pray.

I have learned God is faithful to assist me when I am overwhelmed. When I do not have the ability or skills to solve complicated problems, He gives me needed help.

Every day I pray about my circumstances, and for the

concerns of others. After the loss of my daughter, I experienced support from others to help me get through my grief.

Paul wrote in 2 Corinthians 1:9, "Indeed, we felt that we had received the sentence of death. But that was to make us rely not on ourselves but on God who raises the dead." I, too, felt the pain of death, but also experienced God's goodness. He comforted me as I grieved, as well as strengthened me in my weakness.

Restoration may not require a physical recovery, or a dramatic change of circumstances. When God restored me, He did not change my circumstances. Instead, He changed my outlook.

Jesus motivates and strengthens me to persevere through my hardships. He reduced my emotional pain as the Holy Spirit assured me of Christ's deliverance.

When I fail to obey God because of my stubborn pride and selfishness, I usually fall into deep despair. My dissatisfaction and sorrow make me miserable. As I grieved my daughter's death God helped me to recognize my need for restoration. Since I loved her and missed her so much, a change needed to happen within me.

My faith in God and assurance of His love caused me to seek Him. He enabled me to experience Him as I desired to know His presence with me.

God decreased my sorrow as I became more aware of how He interacts with me. I recognized and accepted His ability to get me through my difficulties. My sorrow lessened as I let Him comfort me.

LISTEN TO THE RIGHT VOICE

I grieve the fact my life will never be the same without my daughter. Bonnie played a huge part in my life. She brought me great joy and provided insightful viewpoints which helped me better understand important matters.

Even though she is now gone, her life continues to cause me to be aware of the concerns of others. Bonnie lived a life of hope in God's grace. I am grateful how she developed her own deep faith in Jesus Christ while she lived her brief time on earth.

As I grieve my loss, God's Spirit makes me aware of my need to be vigilant. Many thoughts enter my mind every day. Some thoughts are not helpful.

I watched old Warner Brothers cartoons with Bonnie. Many times, a cartoon character found himself in a difficult situation. Sometimes when a decision had to be made, two spiritual voices spoke to the troubled cartoon character.

These voices were portrayed as a demon on one shoulder and an angel on the other. One provided heartless advice while the other gave helpful counsel. The rebellious, self-centered cartoon character always chose the bad advice and never got what he wanted.

The cartoon showed there are dishonest messages motivated by selfish gain and self-satisfaction. At first the idea appears to be good, but the thought leads to emptiness and displeasure in the end.

God's Word is referred to as a spiritual light in the darkness and a source of strength for all who obey Him. When I fail to obey God because of my stubborn pride and selfishness, I become miserable.

After Bonnie died, I realized the tighter I held on to what I had lost, the greater my grief. I needed dependable guidance to help me navigate through my sorrow.

BEYOND MY UNDERSTANDING

When feeling the sadness of grief, I get sidetracked and struggle to take God at His Word. I want to place complete trust in Him, but sadness can overwhelm me.

The inner compass I depend on can get badly damaged. When confusion and insecurity cause me to doubt God, I need to reconnect with Him.

The ability to discern and comprehend God's direction is found in the Holy Bible. As I study the Bible, I am reminded to obey His Word and not make stupid choices or compromise my faith.

For example, the Israelites requested protection from their unbelieving neighbors. They did not depend on God. When my focus is not on God, I also allow earthly concerns to control me, and I make poor decisions.

I have heard people say, "Some people are so heavenly minded they are no earthly good." This upsets me because there is no biblical reference to support that comment.

Jesus instructs me to desire the things of heaven, rather than earthly possessions. Matthew 6:21 says, "For where your treasure is, there your heart will be also."

I lost a great treasure here on earth when Bonnie died. Then I recognized my failure to appreciate the reality of heaven and the time we had together. Bonnie now lives with God and is taken care of by Him.

As I trust God and rest in His love, He comforts me. Like John 16:22 says, "So also you have sorrow now, but I will see you again, and your hearts will rejoice, and no one will take your joy from you."

My time of grief helped me develop a hopeful outlook. I now have more compassion for those who suffer. No longer do I depend on my own understanding. Instead, I trust in God.

Jeremiah 9:23-24 reminds me, "Thus says the LORD, 'Let not the wise man boast in his wisdom, let not the mighty man boast in his might, let not the rich man boast in his riches, but let him who boasts boast in this, that he understands and knows me, that I am the LORD who practices steadfast love, justice, and righteousness in the earth. For in these things I delight, declares the LORD.'"

I learned my need to faithfully obey God. He is holy. Without Him, I am lost, and no one on earth can save me.

PREPARATION FOR CONFLICT

I knew about security threats when I served in the Armed Forces. Advanced preparation prior to a conflict helped me to be battle ready. If an unexpected attack happened, my life, as well as the lives of my fellow airmen, would be in danger.

I would not have time to think about what my response would be in an intense, hostile environment. My awareness of a potential tragedy allowed me to be prepared for an attack.

I needed to keep my actions and emotions under control. Otherwise, the possibility of additional harm to myself, or others could happen because of my inability to respond in an appropriate manner.

Preparation exercises helped remind me of my need to be a disciplined, dedicated team member who could be depended upon. I could not let outside distractions or intensity of the battle prevent me from fulfilling my mission. I needed to always be vigilant.

My awareness of a possible ambush could impact my fate, as well as those I am committed to protect. This causes me to always be on guard. Thankfully, I never had to apply what I learned from my military instruction, but my readiness for conflict keeps me alert.

I appreciate how King David conducted himself when he engaged the enemy. He usually prayed for God's direction and help. God often responded in a clear and direct way. David knew what needed to be done in the heat of battle.

As I go through my own hardships, David's example inspires me to not be influenced by a misguided perspective. I do not want to be motivated by emotions. Rather, I want to respond in an appropriate manner as God desires.

I relate to King David when he humbly prayed for his son's life before his child died. He trusted God to do a miracle. David mourned over the terrible condition of this child.

When he learned about his child's death, David ate to restore his physical strength. Then he went to comfort his wife who grieved over her deceased child. A husband needs to support and love his wife.

When I served in the Armed Forces, the term "military bearing" entered my vocabulary. This meant I needed to see beyond myself to assist another in need.

Circumstances should not impair my judgment. I appreciate how God helps me through my unpleasant situations.

I am also grateful how the Holy Spirit has comforted me and turned my sorrow into joy. This happens when I follow the advice of Philippians 4:6-7 which says, "do not be anxious about anything, but in everything by prayer and supplication with thanksgiving let your request be made known to God. And the peace of God, which surpasses all understanding, will guard your hearts and minds in Christ Jesus."

God revealed Himself to me through the peace He gave me after my daughter's death. He allowed me to think clearly and be more aware of the beauty around me.

In the military, I learned the importance of not allowing anyone to be left behind enemy lines. Everyone needs to get out safely. Serious casualties can happen along the way but should not hinder the rescue of those who need help.

My faith in God helps me to remember He is the final authority here on earth. As a veteran I recognize the humility recorded in Matthew 8:5-13. A Roman centurion requested Jesus to heal his sick servant. The centurion commanded 100 Roman soldiers and had authority over them.

Nonetheless, the centurion confessed his unworthiness as he asked Jesus to do a miracle on his behalf. He expressed no arrogance before Christ, even though his position gave him great power over many people.

I never ruled over others as the centurion did, but as an enlisted airman I needed to obey the commands of my superiors. This required me to respect those in authority and set aside my stubborn pride to do what I was told.

Jesus chose to heal the centurion's servant. But neither King David's child nor my daughter received the desired physical healing. Still, God is ultimately in control, and I am in no position to demand what God should or should not do.

I had never experienced such great emotional anguish as I suffered after Bonnie's death. My childhood upbringing and military experience influenced the way I grieve. My source of strength is God who has been a dependable anchor through my terrible hardships.

I confess what Job 19:25 declares, "I know my Redeemer lives." I have trusted Jesus Christ to rescue me in my lost condition, and He provides all I need to persevere through my life and loss.

HOPE IN GOD'S SALVATION

Scripture records how Isaiah and Jeremiah reflected upon their grief and sadness as they observed people in bondage. They wrote between 740 BC and 700 BC, a time when the Israelites were slaves under Babylonian captivity.

Since my daughter died, I, too, am more aware of those struggling with hardship. Emotional pain and disappointment due to my personal loss has heightened my awareness of others who suffer. Like the Hebrew prophets, I trust God to comfort and restore those who go through deep sorrow.

Second Corinthians 10:3-5 reminds me, "For though we walk in the flesh, we are not waging war according to the flesh. For the weapons of our warfare are not of the flesh but have divine power to destroy strongholds. We destroy arguments and every lofty opinion raised against the knowledge of God, and take every thought captive to obey Christ."

I refuse to believe the lies spread by deceptive people which cause fear and confusion. My happiness is not dependent on the limits and restraints placed upon me. The contentment I experience comes from my close relationship with Christ. He has transformed me and changed the way I think and act.

After Bonnie died, I lost an irreplaceable person in my life. Years after her death, I still mourn my loss. I miss her profound insights, and the love she displayed.

My loss is enormous, but her death has confirmed Christ's redemption upon my life. Jesus has helped me overcome my discouragement and despair. This has produced an expectant hope within me.

Psalm 56:13 says, "For you have delivered my soul from death." Jesus has transformed my life and given me eternal life with Him.

My hope is not found in some wishful desire about a possible outcome. Rather, I am certain of God's salvation given to me by Christ. He has restored my life and changed my hopeless outlook. He has taken me out of the darkness of sorrow and brought me into His glorious light.

Early in Christ's ministry, many people watched Him do great miracles. Gradually, a great number who once followed Jesus, became discouraged and departed from Him.

Jesus observed this and asked His disciples, "'Do you want to go away as well?' Simon Peter answered Him, 'Lord to whom shall we go? You have the words of eternal life, and we have believed, and have come to know, that you are the Holy One of God'" (John 6:67-69). I also know Jesus is my only hope, so I put my trust in Him.

I am sad Bonnie's physical restoration did not happen. Nevertheless, I know Jesus Christ has the power to heal and save those who trust Him as their Lord and Savior.

There is no other source of eternal life apart from Jesus Christ. So, daily I expectantly wait upon Him to restore, renew, and heal me of my sorrow.

Like a deep physical wound, grief can take a long time to heal. Every day I put on the spiritual armor of God mentioned in Ephesians 6:10-18 to have His strength and protection in my life.

My irreplaceable loss is a constant reminder for me to grieve with the anticipation of God's restoration. My human pride has been humbled by God. He is faithful to strengthen and empower me.

I do not grieve like others who have no hope. Rather, in my sorrow, I believe God's promises given to me through His trustworthy Word.

HELPFUL PROMISES AND ENCOURAGEMENT WHEN IN GRIEF

"So Jacob called the name of the place Peniel, saying, 'For I have seen God face to face, and yet my life has been delivered'" Genesis 32:30.

"Though he slay me, I will hope in him; yet I will argue my ways to his face" Job 13:15.

"So Samuel told him everything and hid nothing from him. And he said, 'It is the LORD. Let him do what seems good to him'" 1 Samuel 3:18.

"For God alone, O my soul, wait in silence, for my hope is from him. He only is my rock and my salvation, my fortress; I shall not be shaken. On God rests my salvation and my glory; my mighty rock, my refuge is God" Psalm 62:5-7.

"When my soul was embittered, when I was pricked in heart, I was brutish and ignorant; I was like a beast toward you. Nevertheless, I am continually with you; you hold my right hand. You guide me with your counsel, and afterward you will receive me to glory. Whom have I in heaven but you? And there is nothing on earth that I desire besides you. My flesh and my heart may fail, but God is the strength of my heart and my portion forever" Psalm 73:21-26.

"And the LORD will guide you continually and satisfy your desire in scorched places and make your bones strong; and you shall be like a watered garden, like a spring of water, whose waters do not fail" Isaiah 58:11.

"Surely he has born our griefs and carried our sorrows" Isaiah 53:4.

"Blessed are those who mourn, for they shall be comforted" Matthew 5:4.

"Truly, truly, I say to you, you will weep and lament, but the world will rejoice. You will be sorrowful, but your sorrow will turn into joy" John 16:20.

"May the God of hope fill you with all joy and peace in believing, so that by the power of the Holy Spirit you may abound in hope" Romans 15:13.

CHAPTER 11
LOVE

"Love bears all things, believes all things, hopes of things,
endures all things."
1 Corinthians 13:7

When Karen and I raised Bonnie, my parental responsibility focused on the development of her relationship with God. I knew my life would be an example to her of how to love in a godly way.

I am grateful love is the first fruit of God's Spirit. Godly love does not happen naturally. To do what 1 Corinthians 13:7 says is a challenge, especially when hardships arise. A close relationship with God is necessary to learn to love as He desires. God's love bears, believes, hopes and endures all things.

I think back on the times when Bonnie watched me closely. As she did, Bonnie gained confidence in her ability to apply God's Word in practical ways.

Whenever Bonnie and I watched a television program together, I made the effort to ask what she learned from the show. Afterword we frequently talked about what we observed.

As we reflected and expressed our thoughts, she developed discernment.

Our family picked up quotes from some movies we watched frequently. Most of the time they were funny comments. Later, when an embarrassing or difficult circumstance arose in our own lives, we would quote a line from a favorite movie. Immediately we all knew how it related to our situation.

I have learned love is best expressed with kind words. As Proverbs 16:24 says, "Gracious words are like a honeycomb, sweetness to the soul and health to the body." My actions and behavior should match the words I speak.

STAY IN TOUCH

After Bonnie died, I kept in touch with several of her classmates. Some of them expressed frustration with guys their age who found it hard to communicate on a deep personal level.

Their concerns are much like the distant relationship I had with my earthly father. Few people want a spouse or close friends who refuse to open their souls to them.

The pain of my daughter's death caused a disconnection between me and God. I trusted Him to heal Bonnie, but it did not happen. My expectations and hopes were crushed. When I recognized my separation from God, His undeniable, steadfast love held me up when my human strength failed.

Love can remove barriers I put in place to protect myself in relationships. When I am deeply hurt by others, my guard goes up. Emotional walls are quickly built to prevent additional pain.

When I am irritated my natural response is to raise up protective measures and stop communication with others. Some people block phone numbers, defriend others on social media, or ignore the person altogether. These actions are often done in an unkind and insensitive manner.

After I invited Jesus into my life, I did not become perfect. Actually, I will never be perfect here on earth. I need to remember what Paul wrote in 1 Timothy 1:15, "The saying is trustworthy and deserving of full acceptance, that Christ Jesus came into the world to save sinners, of whom I am the foremost."

I daily follow Jesus but am aware of my imperfections. Yet as I grow in Him, His holiness becomes more evident in me.

Christ's love comforts me, and gives me assurance that God accepts me as I am. I do not need to prove myself to God before my life is made right with Him. The work of Jesus Christ's death on the cross is what makes me right with God.

Ephesians 2:8-9 says, "For by grace you have been saved through faith. And this is not your own doing; it is the gift of God, not a result of works, so that no one may boast."

I was profoundly hurt by Bonnie's death. My efforts to keep others at a distance failed when God's love penetrated my broken heart. As Psalm 56:13 says, "For you have delivered my soul from death, that I may walk before God in the light of life."

After Bonnie's death, life was like a long hard winter for me. Trees appear to be lifeless before the warmth of spring reaches their roots. The forest gets rejuvenated with new life when spring arrives.

Like the trees in a forest, I had a long winter season of not realizing God's love for me. A long time passed before I began to praise God for His goodness to me.

As Isaiah 55:12 says, "For you shall go out in joy and be led forth in peace; the mountains and the hills before you shall break forth into singing, and all the trees of the field shall clap their hands." I now deeply appreciate God's great love for me through each passing season of life.

LOVE AND MARRIAGE

My wife and I have been married more than forty years. Not all those years were filled with happiness. There were missed opportunities, unmet expectations, and deep disappointments. Through those difficult days, prayer, hope, commitment and perseverance got us through times of isolation.

The Bible has been our steadfast anchor through our stormy circumstances. Every day we read God's Word together. Then we pray with each other and ask God to help us through the day.

Daily we make an effort to build up and strengthen one another. We recognize our differences. An old proverb says, "opposites attract." Even though we think and act differently, we assure each other of our love.

Our love is motivated by our relationship with God. We are content with one another because our goal is to honor Christ through our lives.

Discouragement, pride, anger, ungodly thoughts, and a detached relationship with God are the main reasons we encounter struggles in our marriage. An unpleasant memory, lack of attention, or tiredness can also hinder my ability to respond in love.

Whenever I find myself critical of Karen, the Holy Spirit helps me to consider my behavior. Often, my problem is not due to her, but rather an insecurity or frustration within me.

Honest communication with God is necessary to calm my troubled soul. Otherwise, problems grow larger without Him. This is when God's love becomes so important. As I focus on what is honest and true, God's love in me controls my emotions when I get annoyed.

God's love helps me to cope with my difficulties. Time and again, He reveals His insights to me. The Holy Spirit then enables me to respond in love rather than find fault with others. He helps me to forgive myself and others when I am frustrated.

Psalm 138:8 is a constant reminder of my need for God's undeserved kindness. "The LORD will fulfill his purpose for me; your steadfast love, O LORD, endures forever. Do not forsake the work of your hands." I am thankful that God continues to mold me into His image.

My facial expressions and responses reveal the discontentment others see in me. When my responses criticize others, I need to evaluate myself.

As Jesus said in Matthew 7:4-5, "how can you say to your brother, 'Let me take this speck out of your eye,' when there is the log in your own eye. You hypocrite, first take the log out of your own eye, and then you will see clearly to take the speck out of your brother's eye."

Disapproval and blame result from my stubborn pride. I must not shield myself from this painful truth. On the other hand, when I intentionally remember God's love for me, I become less defensive.

My deep emotional pain after Bonnie's death could have driven Karen and I apart. Our broken lives needed God's help.

The mutual commitment to keep our marriage vow, "until death do us part," encouraged us to be patient, and trust one other. Many times, I found it difficult to give or receive love when I felt deeply hurt. My need for God's help was vital when loneliness caused me to isolate myself from Karen.

We have intentionally chosen never to have a close physical relationship with anyone outside of our marriage. Proverbs 6:32 says, "He who commits adultery lacks sense; he who does it destroys himself." There are consequences to our actions.

I am grateful how many families, friends, and neighbors supported us in times of need. We are forever thankful for the compassionate expressions of love we received through that miserable experience of losing our daughter.

UNEXPECTED COMPANIONS

Bonnie became concerned when she realized we would need to move to Indiana for several months. Bonnie was worried that we, her parents, would not have friends nearby to support us. The small community where we live has helped us through many hardships.

Neighbors assisted us in every way possible during Bonnie's cancer treatments. Several offered to keep watch over our home while we were away in Indiana. Others provided prayer and financial assistance. Their help provided encouragement when we were overwhelmed with our situation.

We knew the importance of supportive love in a strange new place. Therefore, before we went to Indiana, I contacted my corporate office. I informed the personnel director of our situation. He then provided the names of people in the area where Bonnie's treatment would take place, who might be able to help us.

My employer also asked a medical doctor in the area to be available to assist us. She attended our first appointments with Bonnie's radiation and chemo doctors. This was a great help as we were overwhelmed with our circumstances.

Our acquaintance soon became a trusted friend and committed to meet with us weekly during our time in Indiana. Her presence gave us great comfort.

We were surprised when she brought another doctor with her on her weekly visits. They both lived in the same city. Together they made a weekly two-hour round-trip journey to support our family through Bonnie's cancer treatments. As a result of their long drives together, they developed a close friendship with each other.

These two medical doctors were dependable encouragers, especially for Bonnie and Karen. Their willingness to give unconditional and sacrificial support provided much-needed female companionship for them. Together they focused on how my daughter and wife held up through the stressful weeks of treatment.

I had the opportunity to meet with several pastors throughout the weeks in Indiana. Because of the unpredictable treatment schedule, chemo had to be administered at a precise time prior to the proton radiation. Bonnie could not eat for three hours before the daily radiation either. This prevented Karen and Bonnie from attending my visits with the ministers.

I did my best to provide encouragement and support to my family. Yet I could not provide the feminine companionship Karen and Bonnie needed.

I enjoyed watching the doctors interact with Bonnie and Karen as they supported them. Their lively conversations with each other made me smile. Then I noticed how each doctor had their own unique personality. One doctor is serious like my wife, Karen, the other is funny like Bonnie.

These two very special companions communicated sincere love to us during our time away from home. Their cheerful personalities helped renew our hearts with joy and gladness as Bonnie went through radiation.

After Bonnie's death, we stayed in touch and occasionally visited one another. We have seen God's deep love displayed through their lives.

DIFFERENT TYPES OF LOVE

The unexpected compassion shown by the medical doctors made me aware of how love is shown in different ways. I can have love for a person, a special place, or a favorite sports team.

I have great affection for the two medical doctors who became special friends to my family. Their supportive church also rallied around us and showed us great love. They assisted us through our difficult time in practical ways. Their worship services encouraged us. They prayed for our situation. They displayed their compassion through their gifts and financial support. They also provided meals and a place to stay.

Love can also be thought of in romantic terms. Passionate love should be reserved for marriage to establish a close relationship with one's spouse.

Genesis 2:18 is true. "The LORD God said, 'It is not good that the man should be alone; I will make him a helper fit for him.'" Karen is indeed my helper as she unselfishly supports me through her love.

Her gentleness and companionship have been an immeasurable blessing to me. Together we support one another in love.

This is why Ephesians 5:31 says, "Therefore a man shall leave his father and mother and hold fast to his wife, and the two shall become one flesh." We are united in our effort to honor God.

Karen and I intentionally live in obedience to God's Word. Our actions and words are meant to encourage one another. As Proverbs 16:20 says, "Whoever gives thought to the word will discover good, and blessed is he who trusts in the LORD." Christ's example also motivates me to love others in a godly way.

As Romans 12:9-10 says, "Let love be genuine. Abhor what

is evil; hold fast to what is good. Love one another with brotherly affection. Outdo one another in showing honor."

My love is to be demonstrated with compassion. For example, 1 Corinthians 13 and Proverbs 31:10-31 provide insight into the importance of devotion to God, and those He puts in my life. When love is shown in a meaningful way a genuine regard for one another develops.

I am grateful for the many ways 1 can express love. Since Bonnie's death I have been more intentional to express concern and compassion to those in grief.

My ability to love in a sincere way after my daughter's death did not come naturally. I prefer to keep my distance from painful circumstances and events. Nevertheless, as God strengthens me in my weakness, I am mindful of others who struggle. As 1 Corinthians 12:26 says, "If one member suffers, all suffer together; if one member is honored, all rejoice together."

The God of all comfort has taught me how to live in His love. God has helped me show compassion in genuine ways. In the past I usually gave a hollow, unsympathetic response, to someone who grieved.

It took time for me to learn how to support someone in need. I now understand the importance of compassion. My dependence on God through my hardship has increased my faith in Him. This has enabled me to be more compassionate to others as well.

Over many decades I found Psalm 9:9-10 to be an affirmation of God's goodness in troublesome times. "The Lord is a stronghold for the oppressed, a stronghold in times of trouble. And those who know your name put their trust in you, for you, O LORD, have not forsaken those who seek you."

NECESSARY SUPPORT

After Bonnie died, I became aware of how my behavior rarely showed Christ's love and kindness. I lacked enthusiasm and kept myself away from others.

My work supervisor recognized my behavior. He had another coworker meet with me every two weeks. Our telephone visits helped me improve my outlook as I met with him for over two years.

I do not recall any drastic change in me from those discussions with my coworker. However, over time I gradually developed a new perspective. When we got together, he always wanted to hear from me what I learned from God through my struggle.

I am grateful how God's Word showed me that every great man in the Holy Bible went through difficult times. God also revealed how He helps those who seek Him.

For example, Moses wandered forty years in a desert, Elijah fled in fear from Jezebel's threats, David ran away from King Saul, angels ministered to Jesus after a forty day fast, and Paul needed to go into a barren place before God prepared him to be a leader. Yet, every one of these men understood God works in powerful ways on behalf of those who trust Him.

My need to wait and persevere has produced a long-desired outcome. More than eleven years passed from the time I began to write this book until the time it got published. Philippians 1:6 encouraged me to remain faithful to God's plan. "And I am sure of this, that he who began a good work in you will bring it to completion at the day of Jesus Christ."

Throughout the development of this book, I wanted it done as soon as possible. However, I gained insights from God's Word and others through the writing process. Scripture references helped me to understand how unexpected situations affected my life.

I often got frustrated because it took such a long time for this book to develop. For years people have expressed a desire to read this book. However, all I could give them was my pledge to complete it.

God showed me through Scripture how His people need to support others in difficult times. Moses had Joshua to support him. Elijah had Elisha, David had Jonathan, Christ's disciples had Jesus, and Paul had Barnabas. Each of them received support to persevere through the help of their companions.

Philippians 4:13-14 says, "I can do all things through him who strengthens me. Yet it was kind of you to share my trouble." Because people prayed and encouraged me, I finally finished this long-awaited book.

I am grateful for the many people who encouraged me through this process. My wife Karen, coworkers, and others helped me to finish what I began. They patiently waited for me to complete this book. More importantly, their love gave me needed comfort in my heartbroken condition.

A DEPENDABLE GUIDE

From the day I invited Jesus into my life, He has helped me to know Him better. Jesus has taken me from spiritual darkness to where I now live in His love.

Every day since Jesus saved me, my relationship with God grows deeper. I have an obvious awareness of how His Holy Spirit is at work in me.

Jesus said in John 14:15-17, "If you love me, you will keep my commandments. And I will ask the Father, and he will give you another Helper, to be with you forever, even the Spirit of truth, whom the world cannot receive, because it neither sees him nor knows him. You know him, for he dwells with you and will be in you." My ability to love is a direct result of the Holy Spirit who lives within me.

God the Father, His Son Jesus Christ, and the Holy Spirit work together as a divine threesome. The Holy Spirit must never be referred to as an 'it.' The Holy Spirit is God's representative on earth. He becomes known by every believer who has invited Jesus into their life.

Love displays God's character. As 1 John 4:16 says, "So we have come to know and to believe the love that God has for us. God is love, and whoever abides in love abides in God, and God abides in him."

Instead of a hard heart toward God and others, I have been given a heart of flesh filled with a love to serve Him. As God said in Ezekiel 36:26-27, "And I will give you a new heart, and a new spirit I will put within you. And I will remove the heart of stone from your flesh and give you a heart of flesh. And I will put my Spirit within you, and cause you to walk in my statutes and be careful to obey my rules." I am grateful for the Holy Spirit in my life. He has transformed me and been my dependable guide.

AN UNEXPECTED LOVE

After we returned from Indiana, life went on as normal for several months. Later, Bonnie began to experience physical weakness and paralysis. She fell several times and became unable to walk. She was admitted to the hospital in New York. Bonnie received therapy several times a day. Instead of getting stronger her body continued to get weaker.

After three weeks in the hospital, Bonnie became totally paralyzed. Her body could not respond to the tireless efforts of her medical staff. The rehabilitation and neurological personnel were totally devoted to restoring Bonnie's physical body. They were extremely committed to helping her.

When Bonnie could not move any muscles below her neck, she could not do anything for herself. I frequently watched her nurse's debate about who would get to wash, and braid her long brown hair. Everybody sincerely wanted to help her feel special.

An occupational therapist also learned how my daughter enjoyed movies. Her therapist purchased a newly released movie, then brought her DVD player to the hospital and connected it to the television in Bonnie's room. This enabled them to watch the new movie my daughter wanted to see.

The thoughtfulness of her therapist expressed genuine love. This kind and considerate act of compassion gave Bonnie time to be with her new friend.

Karen and I were preoccupied with other concerns. We never thought about Bonnie's need to watch a fun movie with someone. They enjoyed their time together. The movie also helped to take some stress away from Bonnie as she got her mind off her condition for a few hours.

Her therapist only did this once with Bonnie. Yet, I was impressed how after her long day at work, she returned to the hospital in the evening to spend time with my daughter.

On February 14, a group of medical personnel from the rehab and neurology units visited Bonnie after she moved to the cancer floor. They brought her Valentine's Day cards from all the staff who worked in those units. She even got cards from some of the other patients. The hospital staff wanted to express their love and appreciation for her.

The Valentine cards were stuffed into a small "princess" mailbox. The movie characters Bonnie identified with as a child were pictured on the outside of the mailbox. When the box was opened, a familiar love song played to help her celebrate the letters she received.

Karen and I read more than twenty Valentine cards written to Bonnie from the hospital staff. Tears of joy filled Bonnie's eyes as she heard words of encouragement and appreciation for her life.

The staff from the other departments who came to visit Bonnie over their lunch break also put up colorful stickers on her hospital room windows. They hung pink streamers throughout her room. Because of their previous interaction with Bonnie, the hospital staff knew she liked pink. So, they got her a pink blanket, pink socks, a pink neck pillow, and a stuffed dog with pink polka dots. The staff purchased these gifts from their own personal funds to show their deep love for Bonnie.

Bonnie's aunt lived over two hours away. She and her two young children came to visit. They arrived during this party for Bonnie put on by the hospital staff. They were amazed by the display of compassion for my daughter. The staff felt Bonnie's critical condition warranted their outpouring of love. This memorable Valentine's Day, filled with love, provides me great joy to this day.

A MESSAGE OF HOPE

One day a young nurse who appeared to be Bonnie's age, unexpectedly entered my daughter's room to play her guitar and sing.

The songs she sang were not familiar to us, but her care and concern for Bonnie expressed a sacrificial love. Her music lifted our discouragement and brought us needed hope. This stranger came to bless Bonnie and encourage her in her difficult situation.

This nurse's act of love reminded me how God sent angels

to the shepherds to tell them about Jesus' birth. The angels' message of hope brought encouragement to the shepherds as they watched their flocks at night. The angels' message inspired the shepherds to go see the Savior who had been born into our world.

When I visited the Shepherd's Field in Bethlehem, I needed to walk through a cemetery. The cemetery has a small chapel with paintings to remember the miraculous birth of Jesus Christ. The angels are portrayed as brilliant messengers who came to give the news to the shepherds.

To have been in the place where such an important event happened humbled me. Now, when I visit a cemetery, I am reminded how life is very brief. I look forward to the day when Jesus takes me to my eternal home in heaven, yet I am also grateful for how He is with me here on earth.

As Psalm 56:13 says, "For you have delivered my soul from death, yes, my feet from falling, that I may walk before God in the light of life." Jesus has saved me from death and reveals God's awesome love through His Word.

I am grateful how God used the hospital staff to give me a message of hope. My family witnessed many displays of love in the hospital before Bonnie died. Their compassion comforted us in our time of need.

LOVE DISPLAYED IN LOSS

Moments after Bonnie died, several nurses came into her room. They all had tears running down their faces. Then a friend who sat with us invited everyone to gather around Bonnie.

We held hands with one another as my friend prayed a prayer of thanksgiving for Bonnie's life. Everyone was sad, but grateful she no longer struggled here on earth. God received her into heaven as His greatly loved child.

After his prayer the nurses went back to their stations. Those who were with us then helped to clean Bonnie's room. They gathered all the cards, Valentine decorations, flowers, balloons, stuffed animals, and other items given to Bonnie during her hospital stay.

I was the last person to leave Bonnie's room. I did not want to leave her side, but knew it was necessary.

On my way out, a nurse stopped me before I reached the elevator. He wanted me to know how patients like Bonnie reminded him of why he became a nurse. I kindly thanked him for his care of my daughter, and then departed.

Days later I asked myself, "Why did the nurse think that way?" As a slow processor I often lose opportunities to learn important information from others. My brain often does not react quickly.

Then I thought about the way Bonnie lived her life. She always wanted to show love to everyone. Bonnie naturally let others know her appreciation when they assisted her.

Bonnie's doctors, nurses, therapists, technicians, even service staff who cleaned her room or delivered her meals heard her say "thank you" for their help. Her words were sincere and appreciated by others.

A week after her death, many hospital staff, who had cared for Bonnie, made the hour and a half drive to attend her funeral. Even after her death they displayed their deep dedication to my daughter.

With God's help, I eventually broke out of my loneliness and sorrow. As Jesus said in John 16:20, "You will be sorrowful, but your sorrow will turn into joy." God's love, shown through others, helped me to recover after my great loss.

God's love has freed me from my dark thoughts and anxieties. He has given me renewed hope and the ability to face my trials. His love has transformed my outlook.

Even though I permanently lost an important person in my life, I live with intentional purpose every day. God wants to use me here on earth to honor Him. The best way to show my appreciation for God's kindness to me, is to love others.

God's love empowers me to have faith to persevere through all things. As I hope for the best, and endure my hardships, His love motivates me to honor Him. Through Christ's love I gain endurance to persevere through hardship. I also experience His immeasurable compassion for me.

ENCOURAGEMENT AND PROMISES ABOUT GOD'S LOVE

"The steadfast love of the LORD never ceases; his mercies never come to an end; they are new every morning; great is your faithfulness. The LORD is my portion, says my soul, therefore I will hope in him" Lamentations 3:22-24.

"Because your steadfast love is better than life, my lips will praise you" Psalm 63:3.

"The LORD will fulfill his purpose for me; your steadfast love, O LORD, endures forever. Do not forsake the work of your hands" Psalm 138:8.

"'With everlasting love I will have compassion on you' says the LORD, your Redeemer" Isaiah 54:8.

"I have loved you with an everlasting love; therefore I have continued my faithfulness to you" Jeremiah 31:3.

"This is my commandment, that you love one another as I have loved you" John 15:12.

"For I am sure that neither death nor life, nor angels nor rulers, nor things present nor things to come, nor powers, nor height nor depth, nor anything else in all creation, will be able to separate us from the love of God in Christ Jesus our Lord" Romans 8:38-39.

"So that Christ may dwell in your hearts through faith—that you, being rooted and grounded in love, may have strength to comprehend with all the saints what is the breadth and length and height and depth, and to know the love of Christ that surpasses knowledge, that you may be filled with all the fullness of God" Ephesians 3:17-19.

"In this the love of God was made manifest among us, that God sent his only son into the world, so that we might live through him" 1 John 4:9.

"Above all, keep loving one another earnestly, since love covers a multitude of sins" 1 Peter 4:8.

CHAPTER 12
MERCY

"Blessed be the God and Father of our Lord Jesus Christ!
According to his great mercy, he has caused us to be born again
to a living hope through the resurrection of Jesus Christ from
the dead"
1 Peter 1:3.

Ever since Bonnie died, the reality of Christ's resurrection gives
me an anticipation of an awesome life to come. My hope is not
wishful thinking, but rather God's promise to provide me
eternal life.

Jesus lives at the right hand of God in heaven. When I pray,
Jesus informs His Father about my concerns. He already knows
my concern, yet God still desires me to ask for His help.

Jesus Christ died for me, Bonnie, and everyone else. There
is nothing I can do on my own to make my life right with God
apart from faith in His Son Jesus Christ.

God's greatest expression of mercy occurred when His Son
died and rose again three days later to save me. My heart broke

when my daughter died. God also must have been incredibly sad when His only Son died by crucifixion on the cross.

I cannot deny the fact Jesus Christ has transformed my outlook. My existence here on earth has totally changed since I have been born again. I once lived as a dead man in rebellion against God, but now I live with purpose to honor Him.

For many years I wondered, "How can Good Friday be considered 'good?'" An innocent man was unjustly, and mercilessly murdered due to false accusations. Then I realized, His sacrificial death provides me the only way to have eternal life. Jesus has given me life today and I will live forever with Him in heaven.

Isaiah 53:7 foretold Christ's death, "He was oppressed, and he was afflicted, yet he opened not his mouth; like a lamb that is led to the slaughter, and like a sheep that before its shearers is silent, so he opened not his mouth." Jesus died a terrible death, but never complained as He was beaten and crucified.

I am grateful for the life Jesus made possible for me. As Psalm 23:6 says, "Surely goodness and mercy shall follow me all the days of my life." Christ's forgiveness is an eternal, undeserved gift of God.

Romans 5:10-11 assures me, "For if while we were enemies we were reconciled to God by the death of his Son, much more, now that we are reconciled, shall we be saved by his life. More than that, we also rejoice in God through our Lord Jesus Christ, through whom we have now received reconciliation." The Father of our Lord Jesus Christ is also my Father in heaven!

God knows me as He watches over my life from heaven. He created me and knows my inability to live as I should. Thankfully, He has authority over me and everything else on earth.

No one has the power to change a life like Christ has done in me. Even though I am still the same person I was at birth,

Christ's mercy has made me a new man. Second Corinthians 5:17 promises, "Therefore, if anyone is in Christ, he is a new creation. The old has passed away; behold, the new has come."

From the day I committed my life to Jesus, God's mercy changed me in unexpected ways. When I invited Jesus into my life, the Holy Spirit changed my old nature and made me a new person.

Colossians 3:5-10 describes what happens when I intentionally give up my old rebellious practices to honor God. He readjusts my behavior, and mercifully oversees what I cannot change on my own. Jesus empowers me to live life as God desires.

Bonnie reflected many of my mannerisms while she lived in this world. This happened because we knew each other very well and shared a close relationship with one another. At times we would communicate with one another without saying a word because of our natural and spiritual connection.

I am grateful for God's mercy because I am never separated from His love. He has taken me out of the pit of despair and given me hope in Him.

WHEN MERCY IS HIDDEN

I do not know why God allows bad things to happen. Troublesome circumstances when left unaddressed can give way to despair. When I feel empty, disheartened, and unproductive, my natural inclination is to do whatever I can to pull myself out of my difficulty. I often fail to ask God for His help as frustration builds within me.

When I recognize my inability to change the situation, I pray and ask God for His help. Insight gained through my trouble helps me to know God better. I pray as David did in Psalm 143:1, "Hear my prayer, O Lord; give ear to my pleas for mercy! In your faithfulness answer me, in your righteousness!"

Most of the time my problems do not magically disappear after I pray. What normally happens is I get a new perspective about what troubles me.

A grateful attitude develops within me as God comforts me. I can be content as the Holy Spirit gives me hope in my difficult circumstance. As Philippians 4:6 says, "Do not be anxious about anything, but in everything by prayer and supplication with thanksgiving let your requests be made known to God."

When I do not get what I want, God mercifully reminds me, I am not alone in my hardship. He wants to help me deal with the problem I am not able to change.

Colossians 3:3 mentions how my life is hidden in Christ. This does not mean God hides Himself from me. Instead, His mercy helps me to trust Him in my hardship.

LOOK FORWARD

My daughter's death impacted me in unexpected and troublesome ways. Yet, the reality of my past, present, and unforeseen future causes me to prepare myself for what is ahead.

As a slow processor, my responses are not always instant. I have recognized how my loss of Bonnie impacted my emotional and physical ability to respond. My response is less certain than it used to be.

I am thankful God has given me the ability to delay my responses. This allows me to process my thoughts before I speak.

Habakkuk 2:3 reminds me, "For still the vision awaits its appointed time; it hastens to the end - it will not lie." God's Word is to be trusted. He will do as He promised in His time.

The short time I wait gives me a chance to think about my condition. The Holy Spirit comforts me from God's Word. He reveals God's desire for me so I can respond with humility and patience.

Romans 12:12 encourages me as I go through hardships. As it says, "Rejoice in hope, be patient in tribulation, be constant in prayer."

Prayer helps me when delays happen. Hope and endurance are gained as I trust Him. God knows what is best for me. He is not obligated to respond in the way I think is appropriate. My perspective is limited and imperfect.

When I am deeply hurt, I think about how Christ suffered for me. His great love motivates me to trust Him. When I am not able to comprehend my troublesome situation, He is faithful to comfort me.

I experienced God's consolation when my first full-time employer asked me to resign from my work in Africa. Thankfully, God provided another organization who enabled my family to return to the country where we had previously served. However, we waited four years before we got back to Africa.

Little did I know in those four years, three of our four parents would die. The unexpected delay allowed Karen and I to provide our parents with much needed assistance in their last years on earth. They also had the opportunity to enjoy their granddaughter, Bonnie Mae.

God also showed me mercy when Bonnie died. He encouraged me to keep my trust in Him. My daughter's death put me in a confused and sorrowful condition. Yet God got me through the dark discouragement I faced.

Through my experiences, I learned to accept His sovereign ways. As Luke 1:78-79 says, "because of the tender mercy of our God, whereby the sunrise shall visit us from on high to give light to those who sit in darkness and in the shadow of death, to guide our feet into the way of peace." Jesus changed my outlook from within as I trusted Him to guide me.

The road to restoration and recovery has taken a long time. Yet I continue to place my faith in Jesus for what is ahead. By doing so He keeps me optimistic instead of pessimistic.

Second Corinthians 12:10 says, "For the sake of Christ, then, I am content with weaknesses, insults, hardships, persecutions, and calamities. For when I am weak, then I am strong." This is especially true as I go through trials. I am reminded of God's faithfulness to rescue me. I am grateful for His help in every aspect of my life.

UNEXPECTED MERCY

When I pray, I expect God to be gracious and answer my prayers. When God's response is not what I hope for, I find it hard to patiently wait and trust Him. I am not a person who intentionally wants to suffer and struggle through life.

Yet, when I go through troublesome circumstances, God is still with me. This is why Romans 5:3-5 says, "we rejoice in our sufferings, knowing that suffering produces endurance, and endurance produces character, and character produces hope, and hope does not put us to shame, because God's love has been poured into our hearts through the Holy Spirit who has been given to us."

Whenever I do not receive what I think I deserve, my desire is to know God better through my hardship. His mercy shows me He is my provider as I have limited financial resources. My low monthly income is a constant concern, but He provides what I need to meet my expenses.

My African brethren have been an inspiration as I serve

God with meager resources. My African coworkers have very little money, but they are joyful.

The reason for their joy comes not from the things they have, but from God's goodness. He is faithful to help them through their difficult situations. As they depend on God, He makes them content.

As Philippians 4:10-12 says, "I rejoiced in the Lord greatly that now at length you have revived your concern for me. You were indeed concerned for me, but you had no opportunity. Not that I am speaking of being in need, for I have learned in whatever situation to be content. I know how to be brought low, and I know how to abound. In any and every circumstance, I have learned the secret of facing plenty and hunger, abundance and need."

The example of my coworkers encourages me to trust God. They are secure, content, and unselfish people. Even though my African friends struggle with their lack of resources, they trust in Christ to help them.

My African friends rely on God. They would rather die than abandon or compromise their faith in Jesus Christ. As Nehemiah 9:31 says, "Nevertheless, in your great mercies you did not make an end of them or forsake them, for you are a gracious and merciful God."

I never heard my coworkers complain about their hardships. Even after loved ones are murdered for their faith or are unjustly persecuted, they merely request prayers to persevere in love for those who have harmed them.

This mindset does not come from a natural human effort, but through the Holy Spirit. He works in the hearts of those who commit their lives to Christ.

God's mercy is abundantly obvious to my African friends as they go through great hardships. Christ's joy in their lives testifies to the Holy Spirit in them. By God's mercy He gives them a supernatural ability to get through difficult circumstances.

After my daughter died, I did not know what to do. James 1:2-3 reminded me, "Count it all joy, my brothers, when you meet trials of various kinds, for you know that the testing of your faith produces steadfastness." I do not always get everything I want, but God is merciful to give me what I need.

I am aware how my selfish insensitive actions have a bad impact on others. My problems are not always because of others or my circumstances. Bad choices and procrastination have also caused me problems.

When King David wrote Psalm 51:1, he confessed his sin before God. David needed God's forgiveness for what he had done to Bathsheba and her husband. He said, "Have mercy on me, O God, according to your steadfast love; according to your abundant mercy blot out my transgressions."

God's mercy is given when I confess my sin to God. Titus 3:5 says, "He saved us, not because of works done by us in righteousness, but according to His own mercy, by the washing of regeneration and renewal of the Holy Spirit." His mercy is not dependent upon my own efforts to please Him.

I am thankful that when I confess my faults before God, He is faithful to forgive me. His mercy stops the cycle of my bad thoughts and actions. Through the Holy Spirit God produces Christ-like character in my life.

God's thoughts are far greater than my own. When I trust Jesus Christ in my difficult and uncertain times, His mercy allows me to experience contentment.

When I go through the storms of life, God protects me from the strong undercurrents I cannot see. Uncertainty, darkness, despair, and disappointment are a reality every day. Thankfully, by Christ's mercy, I have hope for a better tomorrow.

HIS MERCY ALLOWS ME TO PERSEVERE

When Bonnie received cancer treatments, I trusted God to heal my daughter. Briefly her therapy provided signs of recovery, but eventually the tumor grew and took her life.

Through the treatments and her death, God's mercy provided me needed endurance and hope. The best comparison I can give is from my youth when I ran long distance races in high school.

When I ran cross-country races in high school, a sharp pain often occurred under my ribs. The severe discomfort gave me doubts about my ability to finish the race. Internal pain tempted me to give up on my effort to reach the finish line.

I hurt badly inside but kept focused on the goal to complete my race. When I reached the finish line my legs were weak, and I struggled to take a deep breath. The outcome of my efforts usually placed me near the end, even though I never tried to finish last. I always did my best and finished the races. I wanted to prove to myself I could finish what I started.

Jesus said in Matthew 19:30, "but many who are first will be last, and the last first." God's mercy has given me a renewed hope to finish my earthly race. A day is coming when God will reward those who have remained faithful to Him.

Mercy is given when I do not receive what I deserve. Jesus Christ has kept me from the temptation to prematurely quit because of my difficult circumstance. He empowers me to go on even in my weakness. The endurance gained through my miserable experiences has made me stronger.

Ecclesiastes 9:11 reminds me, "Again I saw that under the sun the race is not to the swift, nor the battle to the strong, nor bread to the wise, nor riches to the intelligent, nor favor to those with knowledge, but time and chance happen to them all." God wants me to give Him my woeful condition so He can reveal Himself to me.

I am blessed to know God has authority over all His creation. God loves me so much. He mercifully assists me every day while I go through my struggles. My daughter's death has given me a deep, deep heartache. Yet, God constantly provides the strength and comfort I need to endure my hardships.

UNFORESEEN MERCY

The winter Bonnie died was the coldest we had experienced in many, many years. The ground was so frozen it took three months for it to thaw before we could bury my daughter. The closure I desired was mercifully delayed.

Every day prior to her burial, I remembered our good times together. The reality of my loneliness troubled me. The postponement of her burial also bothered me.

When spring arrived, the scheduled date for Bonnie's burial came a few days before Mother's Day. The day is normally set aside to celebrate life, motherhood, and family. Now every year when May arrives, my thoughts always go back to Bonnie's burial.

Initially I compared the delay of her burial to a bad joke. Little did I know God would provide me unforeseen mercy in the delay. As I waited for Bonnie's burial at the cemetery, I enjoyed the warm spring morning. After a long frigid winter, I realized my heart had become like the frozen ground, cold and hard.

I took note of the fresh new life around me. I looked at plump buds on the trees. The restoration of nature gave me assurance of a transformation soon to come. Colorful wildflowers also emerged from the once lifeless soil.

I heard the music of songbirds. Then I listened to beautiful melodies of violins played by our friends. My dry and calloused soul began to soften.

A dearly loved nephew sat on my knee. We sadly looked at Bonnie's closed casket before us. As we held each other closely, I remembered how my daughter often comforted me in a similar manner with her hugs.

What I experienced at Bonnie's burial serves as a pleasant reminder of how she lived her life. I remember her warmth, vitality, and love. Bonnie had the unique ability to see, hear, and enjoy the smallest details around her. I also noticed the beauty around me that day. I allowed my senses to take in the pleasant sights, smells, and sounds—all of which lifted my downcast soul.

After everyone departed the cemetery, I remained alone at Bonnie's gravesite. I realized this would be the last time I would be physically near to her here on earth. Deep sorrow filled me, but I knew I needed to let go of Bonnie. I trusted my merciful God to keep her in His care until I see her again in heaven.

Jesus not only received my daughter into heaven, but He also took me out of my dark pit. I received the closure I desired when Bonnie was finally buried, and Jesus energized my life in unforeseen ways. I gained a new outlook on life and death.

God caused me to think about how He allowed His only Son to suffer and die. Yet by Christ's resurrection from the dead, I have gained new life through Him. First Peter 1:3 says, "Blessed be the God and Father of our Lord Jesus Christ! According to his great mercy, he has caused us to be born again to a living hope through the resurrection of Jesus Christ from the dead."

My life seemed isolated from God after Bonnie died, but He mercifully reunited me with Himself. He raised me up out of the powerful undercurrent of my sorrow. The Holy Spirit has refreshed my soul, so I am able to appreciate His great love for me once again.

The words of Psalm 40:1-3 reflect my encounter with God's mercy. "I waited patiently for the LORD; he inclined to me and heard my cry. He drew me up from the pit of destruction, out of the miry bog, and set my feet upon a rock, making my steps secure. He put a new song in my mouth, a song of praise to our God. Many will see and fear and put their trust in the LORD."

Years later, I am still sad because I deeply miss my only child. After Bonnie died, I became more sensitive and aware of those who suffer. My discernment causes me to be kinder, humbler, and more patient with those who struggle.

As 2 Corinthians 1:3-4 says, "Blessed be the God and Father of our Lord Jesus Christ, the Father of mercies and God of all comfort, who comforts us in all our affliction, so that we may be able to comfort those who are in any affliction, with the comfort with which we ourselves are comforted by God."

I rest in the fact that God oversees this world. When circumstances seem to be out of control, I do not fear. Rather, I am confident He will keep me in His love and care.

When what I desire does not happen as expected, I look forward to a greater blessing yet to come. God gives me the hope of His ability to make beauty out of ashes. His mercy humbles me.

When life makes no sense, He is still merciful. As Isaiah 40:29 says, "He gives power to the faint, and to him who has no might he increases strength."

GOD'S MERCY PROVIDES RESTORATION

Bonnie's death helped me to experience God in a powerful way. I wanted my daughter to be physically healed. Nevertheless, her death impacted me in unimaginable and wondrous ways.

I never anticipated how my great emotional pain and physical loss would take me into a deeper relationship with God. I am now aware how my hopeless condition, distress, and loss kept me miserable for many years.

When I allowed the bitterness of my loss to deteriorate and weaken me, unexpected consequences occurred. Just as rust and cancer cause great damage when left untreated, my self-centered behavior caused damage within me. The Holy Spirit revealed my selfish motives and kept me from self-destruction.

God's mercy is much more than not receiving what I deserve. Mercy is redemption. God transformed my down-hearted condition. Through the Holy Spirit, He restored me in a miraculous way after my traumatic loss.

Jesus liberated me from my hopeless condition by His once and for all victory over sin and death. He died on a cross for me to be made right with my Heavenly Father.

This is why Romans 12:2 tells me, "Do not be conformed to this world, but be transformed by the renewal of your mind, that by testing you may discern what is the will of God, what is good and acceptable and perfect."

Christ Jesus took my heavy burdens when He rescued me. My own efforts to make myself right before Him were worthless. Only by Christ's sacrifice on the cross am I made right with God.

This is why I rely on Him for a better tomorrow. I do not deserve God's forgiveness given to me through Christ Jesus. Yet He accepts and receives me just as I am, a person who is in desperate need of Him.

God's restorative mercy causes me to rejoice. As 1 Peter 1:3-4 says, "Blessed be the God and Father of our Lord Jesus Christ! According to his great mercy, he has caused us to be born again to a living hope through the resurrection of Jesus Christ from the dead, to an inheritance that is imperishable, undefiled, and unfading, kept in heaven for you."

HELPFUL PROMISES AND ENCOURAGEMENT ABOUT GOD'S MERCY

"The LORD passed before him and proclaimed, 'The LORD, the LORD, a God merciful and gracious, slow to anger, and abounding in steadfast love and faithfulness'" Exodus 34:6.

"When you are in tribulation, and all of these things come upon you in the latter days, you will return to the LORD your God and obey his voice. For the LORD your God is a merciful God. He will not leave you or destroy you or forget the covenant with your fathers that he swore to them" Deuteronomy 4:30-31.

"Then Job answered the LORD and said: 'I know that you can do all things, and that no purpose of yours can be thwarted" Job 42: 1-2.

"Surely goodness and mercy shall follow me all the days of my life" Psalm 23:6.

"Therefore the LORD waits to be gracious to you, and therefore he exalts himself to show mercy to you. For the LORD is a God of justice; blessed are all those who wait for him" Isaiah 30:18.

"The steadfast love of the LORD never ceases; his mercies never come to an end; they are new every morning; great is your faithfulness" Lamentations 3:22-23.

"Thus says the LORD of hosts, Render true judgments, show kindness and mercy to one another" Zechariah 7:9.

"Blessed are the merciful, for they shall receive mercy" Matthew 5:7.

"Behold, we consider those blessed who remain steadfast. You have heard of the steadfastness of Job, and you have seen the purpose of the Lord, how the Lord is compassionate and merciful" James 5:11.

"Once you were not a people, but now you are God's people; once you had not received mercy, but now you have received mercy" 1 Peter 2:10.

"Keep yourselves in the love of God, waiting for the mercy of our Lord Jesus Christ that leads to eternal life. And have mercy on those who doubt; save others by snatching them out of fire; to show mercy with fear" Jude 21-23.

CHAPTER 13
GRACE

"But by the grace of God I am what I am, and his grace toward
me was not in vain"
1 Corinthians 15:10.

Bonnie always desired to stay true to her identity as a young
person who loved Jesus. She lived a modest, quiet, and intentional life of grace.

Throughout high school Bonnie's peers tried to change her
hairstyle, the way she dressed, what she read, and the music she
enjoyed, but their efforts failed. She enjoyed her relationship
with Jesus and did not feel the need to change herself to please
someone else.

Many of her classmates chose to distance themselves from
Bonnie. Her nonconformity caused those students to reject her
as a person because she chose to be different.

Her rejection by others caused my daughter to have some
insecurity and loneliness. Efforts were made to bridge the gaps
in her relationships. We had sleepovers at our home, and

Bonnie got involved in school activities. Sadly, her attempts to develop stronger friendships failed.

Fortunately, many of Bonnie's teachers appreciated her mature attitude and convictions. She was always willing to assist others. One teacher asked her to write notes of encouragement to students who struggled, and to remember her classmates who had a birthday.

Bonnie did this for several years. She never signed her name to a letter. She did not want to draw attention to herself. Nevertheless, everyone knew who wrote the card by her unique handwriting, and the kind words she wrote.

Her effort to be gracious to others did not produce much appreciation. Few acknowledged the kindness given to them. Nonetheless, grace is a free gift that is not deserved. I encouraged Bonnie to keep up her expressions of love, even when the response was not returned in a similar manner.

Bonnie understood the grace of God. She wanted to live her life with compassion and kindness. The Holy Spirit helps believers know their service for God is not in vain.

GRACE AND THE IMPOSSIBLE

God helped Bonnie to be socially mature at a young age. Her experiences with the lack of electricity, water, and phone service were part of everyday life in Africa. Bonnie also knew several students, as well as parents of classmates, who died of sickle cell anemia, accidents, AIDS, or were murdered while she attended primary school.

As a high school student in the United States, she listened to her peers over lunch. Fashion, media, and superficial relationships were their concerns. Bonnie offered little input into their discussions, for their backgrounds were very different.

In her sophomore year, Bonnie enjoyed her role as the

"Fairy Godmother" in the school musical "Cinderella." Bonnie's part began as Cinderella lamented over her stepsisters' and stepmother's unkind words before they attended a royal ball without her.

Moments before Bonnie came on the stage, Cinderella sadly sang about her dreams while she imagined and entertained herself in her own little room. Cinderella's Fairy Godmother then appeared unexpectedly.

Bonnie, as the Fairy Godmother, sang a silly song that did not seem to fit the bad situation. Nonetheless, she got Cinderella's attention and reminded her how impossible circumstances can change every day.

My daughter knew this very well from her own experiences in Africa. On a weekly basis she observed hopeless conditions become transformed supernaturally. God's grace gave people what they needed in their difficult circumstances.

Bonnie's experiences in Africa, the opportunities given her in high school, and the perseverance to accomplish great things through her faith made a tremendous impact upon her life. She knew her accomplishments did not happen because of wealth, wisdom, or social status, but by God's grace.

His grace provided my daughter a chance to experience abundant blessings. Bonnie faithfully acknowledged her need of Christ's grace. She lived to shine God's light in our spiritually dark world.

A WAY OF LIFE

At twenty-two years of age, on a tiny Aleutian Island in Alaska, I asked Jesus to become my Savior and take control of my life. With His help, I have been able to give up my prideful ways to be more gracious in my responses.

Christ's unconditional love helps me to be mindful of

others. As 2 Corinthians 9:8 says, "God is able to make all grace abound to you, so that having all sufficiency in all things at all times, you may abound in every good work." God's grace is needed to live as He desires.

Second Corinthians 6:10 also explains my condition, "as sorrowful yet always rejoicing; as poor, yet making many rich; as having nothing, yet possessing everything." I am blessed by God's kindness which I do not deserve.

My ability to be gracious is not a natural trait, but a God-given gift. God does this so I can know Him in my life. Since Bonnie died, I have been able to reply in a gentler manner to others. My patience is more evident as I no longer try to be first in line. I allow others to move ahead of me.

After Bonnie's death, I received grace from people who cared about me. Their kindness helped me to be mindful of my need to be more gracious to others.

I have found Psalm 55:22 a great comfort as it says, "Cast your burden on the LORD, and he will sustain you, he will never permit the righteous to be moved." God is faithful to provide what I need to rise above my weaknesses, concerns, and fears.

Second Corinthians 1:5 says, "For as we share abundantly in Christ's sufferings, so through Christ we share abundantly in comfort too." My ability to do this is challenged because of my sinful nature.

Anyone, including myself, can fail to accept God's grace and goodness. Pride, selfishness, anger, and deceit are common reasons I fail to accept or appreciate His love for me.

Deuteronomy 11:16 warns how my sinful nature causes me to disobey God. My human nature is influenced by arrogance and ingratitude. The temptation to be thoughtless is an ever-present danger.

When I trust in my own understanding, I am easily led

astray by deceptive lies. The undercurrent of misguided self-reliance causes damage and destructive consequences in my life.

I have witnessed several marriages where a spouse becomes dissatisfied with their husband or wife. The unhappy person selfishly desires sex outside of marriage, pornography, or becomes enslaved to drugs or alcohol to find temporary satisfaction.

When I read the book of Proverbs, I am warned about my natural desire to sin. This is why I intentionally seek to have a close relationship with God. Otherwise, it is easy for me to fall into ungodly behavior.

WHO IS MY GOD?

When worldly passions and desires become more important than God, I become preoccupied with ungodly thoughts. The strong attraction of worldly pursuits can become an idol in my life.

God warns me in the Ten Commandments not to have any other gods before Him (Exodus 20:3). God wants me to totally trust Him and obey His Word. Through Jesus Christ, I am empowered to please God.

Apart from God I naturally do what is wrong. No one other than Christ can give me God's salvation. I have learned the importance of trusting God. This is why Hebrews 10:23 says, "Let us hold fast the confession of our hope without wavering for he who promised is faithful." I am not always faithful, but God is.

When I get insensitive to Jesus, my outlook gets compromised. I become miserable and unhappy about life. My satisfaction and contentment disappear when I lose sight of God's grace.

This is why the writer of Proverbs 3:7-8 says, "Be not wise in your own eyes; fear the LORD, and turn away from evil. It will be healing to your flesh and refreshment to your bones."

When my selfish concerns become more important than God's plan for me, I foolishly get misled. Earthly treasures can keep me from God's intention for my life.

Proverbs 15:13-14 reminds me, "A glad heart makes a cheerful face, but by sorrow of heart the spirit is crushed. The heart of him who has understanding seeks knowledge, but the mouths of fools feed on folly." When Bonnie died my spirit got crushed. I needed to intentionally apply God's Word to my life every day.

When I failed to grasp and appreciate God's grace, I did not have joy. My sadness made me isolate myself from God and others. Thankfully God provided me help and comfort when life appeared hopeless. When I neglected God, I failed to take pleasure in His goodness.

My disconnect from God and others caused me to be discontent, angry, and impatient. Proverbs 14:10 says, "The heart knows its own bitterness, and no stranger shares its joy." Separation ends in sadness.

When I noticed how my thoughts, words, and actions were not gracious, I recognized my lack of compassion toward others. God's grace empowered me to love others. So, I depended upon Him to develop a positive outlook within me.

I deliberately desire to honor God in my thoughts and behavior. Jesus graciously took me out of my darkness into His awesome light.

John 3:21 explains "whoever does what is true comes to the light, so that it may be clearly seen that his works have been carried out in God." Jesus Christ is my Savior and Lord. He takes me out of my hopeless condition as He brings me into His glorious light. By Christ's grace, He transformed my life to honor God.

The disappointments, pain, and frustration from my daughter's death made it difficult to recognize God's grace. Yet I trusted Him to reveal His undeserved kindness to me. Therefore, I now make an intentional effort not to allow bitterness and anger to keep me from God's love. Instead, I daily seek His help.

A MOUNTAIN TO OVERCOME

Matthew 17:20-21 speaks about how a small amount of faith can move huge obstacles. When in Africa, I often experienced God's grace as He kept me from serious harm. My faith in Him grew as He protected me from great dangers. God's protection made the difference between life and death.

Several times a year, my family traveled a narrow, dirt road along a steep mountainside. In the rainy season the roads of clay became slick as ice. There were times my family needed to get out of the heavy Land Rover while our driver maneuvered through a very narrow section of road. He did not want us in the vehicle if a tire failed to hold the road, and we were to tumble down the steep cliff.

We struggled to walk on the slippery mud road. One side of the narrow path provided a rock foundation where some stability could be found. The steep cliff on the other edge of the road dropped hundreds of feet to the valley below. There were no "guard rails" along the passage to keep our vehicle from a disastrous plunge.

By God's grace we completed our journeys safely. We traveled in the days when there were no cell phones or 911 service. More times than my family likes to remember, we viewed lifeless bodies along the roadside who had died in an accident only moments before our arrival.

Faith is what is hoped for but not seen. My family always placed a deep trust in God's grace. We are never guaranteed a life without problems. We daily ask God to help us and pray for His undeserved kindness when hardships arise.

First Corinthians 10:12 warns, "Therefore let anyone who thinks that he stands take heed lest he fall." When I find myself in spiritual darkness due to a hard heart towards God, life becomes very difficult. I needed to recognize my need for God.

When Bonnie's cancer was discovered, my family knew we faced an uphill battle. Perseverance, faith, and endurance were necessary while our daughter battled for her life. Thankfully, we experienced God's kindness through those who helped her.

Bonnie and I did not receive the outcome as we hoped. She did not want to give up her life here on earth. But she went on to her new home in heaven.

Karen rejoiced in the fact our daughter no longer needed to suffer in pain. Bonnie lived a pure and honest life. To see the ungodly behavior and lies accepted in our world today would have broken her heart.

Isaiah 57:1-2 says, "The righteous man perishes, and no one lays it to heart; devout men are taken away, while no one understands. For the righteous man is taken away from calamity; he enters into peace; they rest in their beds who walk in their uprightness." Bonnie now enjoys her new life with God in heaven.

I, on the other hand, continue to learn more about God as He comforts me. My journey on His straight and narrow path unexpectedly took me to the rugged Himalayan Mountains.

SECURE ON AN UNSTEADY COURSE

Three years after Bonnie died, Karen and I went to South Asia for six weeks. Near the world's highest summits, we experienced unexpected adventures. The ancient villages and gigantic mountains provided us with misty views. The clouds and mountain top villages often merged into a thick white fog.

Many places we visited were more than 600 years old. Some communities, located in remote areas, can only be reached on foot.

To reach these villages people walk along steep mountainsides. They use suspension bridges, which cross deep canyons, to reach secluded areas. These bridges have no support underneath them. All you can see as you walk over the bridge is the raging river far below. You can also feel the ice-cold air rise up from the frigid river.

I watched in amazement as local people walked or ran over these bridges without fear. Their confidence on the narrow catwalk reminded me of my own journey with Christ. I had confidence in Christ. But I was afraid to step one foot on that swaying bridge.

Jesus describes life here on earth as a straight and narrow path when we follow Him. He has a destination and purpose for me. God's intention for my life is discovered as I seek Him and obey His Word. As I study the Holy Bible God reveals His desire for me.

After Bonnie died, my unstable path felt like the sway of a suspension bridge. I intended to take care of Bonnie, but I could not prevent her death. I had little confidence in myself. My dilemma put me at risk of a dangerous downfall.

I imagined how difficult it must be to carry a heavy load through a rainstorm on a suspension bridge at night. There is no end in sight, only a passionate motivation in the person that inspires them to reach their destination. These thoughts reflected my condition after Bonnie died. I wanted to be back on solid ground instead of on a swinging bridge.

Thankfully by God's grace, Jesus saved me on my pathway of despair. With the help of the Holy Spirit, I received help with my insecurity. I received direction from God's Word, that provided me inner peace when sorrow overshadowed my perception.

God took me through the shadow of death. Like those who walk over a suspension bridge, I needed to not be afraid about my unstable condition. Yet my loss laid a heavy burden upon me.

I needed to depend upon God and allow Him to help me through this difficult time. As I trusted Jesus, He graciously calmed my insecure and troubled soul. His grace sustained me. As Exodus 14:14 says, "The LORD will fight for you, and you have only to be silent."

DESTRUCTIVE IDOLS

Hinduism and Buddhism are the dominant religions in South Asia. At first, they appear similar, but a closer observation shows differences.

Hinduism has thousands of gods and idols. Hindus believe in Brahma as the creator god, Shiva the destroyer, and Vishnu as their preserver. They offer food, incense, spices, and flowers to their idols. The ring of bells is also a common sound when offerings are made. These offerings are made so the gods will listen to their prayers.

Buddhism on the other hand, does not believe in a creator god. Buddhists seek to overcome suffering through meditation and studying Buddha's teachings. They seek to reach enlightenment or nirvana.

Both religions deny the belief in the One Supreme God of the Bible who created all things and rules over His creation. In Hinduism and Buddhism good fortune depends on an individual completing certain activities. Idols are believed to possess powers. The idols are worshiped to obtain a desired result.

Their practices made me think about how I responded to Bonnie's death. Did I make idols in my own life and neglect God's Word? Did my thoughts and actions honor Him? Or were my efforts to get what I wanted focused on selfish desires?

Jesus asked His disciples in Luke 12:25-26, "And which of you by being anxious can add a single hour to his span of life? If then you are not able to do as small a thing as that, why are you anxious about the rest?" Worry and stress do cause harm. Yet the Bible never tells me to find comfort and wisdom through earthly means.

Instead, I am to learn, follow, and obey God's Word. As I do so, my thoughts change. Desired restoration does not come through my own efforts and strength. My flawed expectations, and unrealistic outlook prevent me from the recognition of God's undeserved kindness to me.

I can choose to make myself judge and jury about what is right and wrong. I do not receive any comfort from my unnecessary self-condemnation. My misguided thoughts have only hindered my appreciation of God's kindness. Therefore, a close relationship with God is necessary to recognize His goodness.

Even though my only child died, God still uses my life to impact others. I noticed how my Asian friends were upset when I departed their country. They did not want me to go. Though we did not have the same faith and could not communicate clearly, we enjoyed being together.

As Acts 20:24 says, "But I do not account my life of any value nor as precious to myself, if only I may finish my course and the ministry that I received from the Lord Jesus, to testify of the gospel of the grace of God." I want my life to impact others in a positive way. As I receive God's undeserved kindness, He allows me to reflect His love and tell others about Christ's salvation so they may know Him.

GRACE BUILDS UP

Psalm 62:1-7 encourages me as I go through hardship. This passage reminds me how God is gracious to me as I trust Him in my struggles. God alone is my dependable help when I experience hardship.

This is why I desire God's assistance. He daily is gracious to renew and redirect my thoughts. My sorrow is turned into joy when I am made aware of His undeserved kindness.

An unexpected change of perspective happened during the COVID-19 pandemic. I called my congressman's office about a concern. At the end of our conversation, the staff person broke down in tears. She said no one had expressed appreciation for her work as I did. When undeserved kindness is given, people are encouraged.

God is gracious to help me every day. So, I trust Him when I am troubled. God said in Jeremiah 33:3, "Call to me and I will answer you, and will tell you great and hidden things that you have not known."

This is why I often humbly talk to God throughout my day. When I consciously quiet myself before Him, He makes known His thoughts about my concerns.

The Spirit of God brings Bible verses to my remembrance to calm my troubled soul. He also gives me courage and His peace to renew my faith in Him.

God graciously gives me hope in His ability to take control over my difficult circumstances. Therefore, I seek to stay optimistic when desired outcomes are not yet seen. As God gives me His undeserved kindness, I can be content with my situation.

Unlike all other world religions, I have no need to gain God's favor before He helps me in my hardship. Through Christ, God allows me to have a personal relationship with Him. He secures my life through His promise to be with me no matter what happens.

Ephesians 3:16-19 reminds me how Jesus strengthens me. I get overwhelmed by the greatness of God's love. I do not understand God's thoughts and intentions in every situation. Yet He provides me needed comfort by His limitless compassion and undeserved kindness.

Indeed, I am what I am by God's undeserved grace. His free gift of salvation graciously enables me to get through each moment of my life.

HELPFUL PROMISES AND ENCOURAGEMENT WHEN IN NEED OF GOD'S GRACE

"He leads me beside still waters. He restores my soul" Psalm 23:3.

"He who dwells in the shelter of the Most High will abide in the shadow of the Almighty. I will say to the LORD, 'My refuge and my fortress, my God in whom I trust'" Psalm 91:1-2.

"Thus says the LORD: 'The people who survived the sword found grace in the wilderness; when Israel sought for rest, the LORD appeared to him from far away. I have loved you with an everlasting love: therefore I have continued my faithfulness to you'" Jeremiah 31:2-3.

"For from his fullness we have all received, grace upon grace. For the law was given through Moses; grace and truth came through Jesus Christ" John 1:16-17.

"Now the law came in to increase the trespass, but where sin increased, grace abounded all the more, so that, as sin reigned in death, grace also might reign through righteousness leading to eternal life through Jesus Christ our Lord" Romans 5:20-21.

"But he said to me, 'My grace is sufficient for you, my power is made perfect in weakness.' Therefore, I will boast all the more gladly of my weaknesses, so that the power of Christ may rest upon me" 2 Corinthians 12:9.

"For by grace you have been saved through faith. And this is not your own doing; it is the gift of God" Ephesians 2:8.

"Therefore, as you received Christ Jesus the Lord, so walk in him" Colossians 2:6.

"He saved us, not because of works done by us in righteousness, but according to his own mercy, by the washing of regeneration and renewal of the Holy Spirit, whom he poured out on us richly through Jesus Christ our Savior, so that being justified by his grace we might become heirs according to the hope of eternal life" Titus 3:5-7.

CHAPTER 14
PEACE

"You have led in your steadfast love the people whom you have redeemed; you have guided them by your strength to your holy abode."

Exodus 15:13

Bonnie's problem of double vision caused my family to go through an unexpected journey. Her unstable balance, and poor vision gave rise to more serious physical challenges. She fought hard through her final summer months to keep herself strong and mobile.

Bonnie received physical, speech, and occupational therapy. The treatments initially helped her regain some skills lost because of the tumor. Thankfully, the proton radiation caused little damage to her organs near the cancerous tissue.

Hopeful signs of recovery through Bonnie's early treatments encouraged everyone. Later, only seven months after college graduation, her entire right side became weak. She began to use a cane and enjoyed Christmas at home. Then her health quickly took a turn for the worse.

Bonnie loved to learn and worked hard to fulfill her academic requirements. However, cancer complications made it impossible to complete her first semester of graduate school.

When Bonnie got admitted to the hospital in mid-January, the neurological unit provided much-needed physical therapy. Unfortunately, day by day, her physical skills diminished.

The medical staff marveled at Bonnie's determination to stay mobile. Her right side was paralyzed so they had her measured for a personal electric wheelchair.

However, within forty-eight hours Bonnie's arm and hand on her left side also became totally paralyzed. This prevented her from using the electric wheelchair, because she could no longer push the controls to make it move.

Yet we were encouraged by those who prayed for her recovery. Heroic efforts were made by the doctors and medical staff to help restore my daughter's health. Around-the-clock care gave me hope her condition would soon improve.

HARD TO SWALLOW

As Bonnie's condition deteriorated, the doctors recommended some additional radiation. This photon radiation caused her throat to become sore. This made swallowing difficult. By the end of February, Bonnie began to receive an IV drip. She could not eat or drink much, so the IV fluid kept her body hydrated.

The normal messages from my daughter's brain to her muscles began to fail, which caused additional problems. She was not allowed to have water because the risk of the liquid entering her lungs could have caused pneumonia.

Bonnie always enjoyed eating a Frosty from Wendy's fast-food restaurant. Karen's sister arrived one day with two Frosty's, one chocolate and one vanilla. This allowed Bonnie to choose which flavor she wanted. After checking with the nurse,

Bonnie received permission to drink the milkshakes. Their thick, dense consistency gave Bonnie's brain time to send the liquid down the proper tube. The milkshakes went into her stomach rather than her lungs.

Since Bonnie had become so hungry, she devoured both Frosty's. Not only did they satisfy her hunger, but it happened to be Bonnie's last meal here on earth.

This experience reminded me of 2 Corinthians 5:4 which speaks about getting rid of our earthly body and taking on our new heavenly body. While I live here on earth, burdens trouble me, and my body gets diseased and becomes weak. But God continues to give me strength. This is why I want to honor Him. I am grateful how Jesus daily restores me in my weak condition.

Second Corinthians 4:16-17 reminds me, "So we do not lose heart. Though our outer self is wasting away, our inner self is being renewed day by day. For this light momentary affliction is preparing us for an eternal weight of glory beyond all comparison." My momentary hardships are worth the wait for a glorious outcome.

God is with me as I go through painful struggles. As Psalm 9:9 says, "The LORD is a stronghold for the oppressed, a stronghold in times of trouble."

First Peter 2:25 also explains why I need God's help. "For you were straying like sheep, but have now returned to the Shepherd and Overseer of your souls." I thank God for how He guides and comforts me.

Jesus wraps His love around me as horrific events, and ungodly policies are forced upon me. Thankfully, God gets me through difficult times. As the caretaker of my soul, He is good to me.

God is my strength when I am weak. He takes care of me in unexpected ways. Just as He provided Bonnie with Frosty milkshakes in her time of need, God daily sustains me in unforeseen circumstances.

MY SOURCE OF SATISFACTION AND PEACE

My work responsibilities require me to travel long distances each year. I hear the struggles and disappointments of those I visit. This gives me opportunity to pray with them, offer support, and give assurance of God's help.

Isaiah 65:24 says, "Before they call I will answer; while they are yet speaking I will hear." God is aware of everyone's concerns while He watches over each person's life. As a believer of Jesus Christ, I have learned to trust God through the chaotic, confused, sad, and difficult times in my life.

After the loss of my only child, I absolutely needed a renewed outlook and purpose in my life. Through the help of the Holy Spirit, God provided me a steadfast determination, and anticipation of His guidance.

I expected God to heal my daughter. Yet when she died, my hope and trust in God temporarily dwindled. My faith grew as I acknowledged God's sovereignty. Sovereignty is the belief that God is free to do anything He chooses, even when I do not understand why bad events happen. My acceptance of His Lordship and my salvation have kept me steadfast in Him.

With a desire for God's inner restoration, I prayed Psalm 51:12, "Restore to me the joy of your salvation, and uphold me with a willing spirit." I asked God to renew my faith with hope. I needed assurance of His care for me in my broken condition.

James 1:5 says, "If any of you lacks wisdom, let him ask God, who gives generously to all without reproach, and it will be given him." God's wisdom is far different from what the world offers me.

This is why Romans 12:2 says, "Do not be conformed to this world, but be transformed by the renewal of your mind, that by testing you may discern what is the will of God, what is good and acceptable and perfect."

Defiance against God and His Word motivates unsatisfied people to find happiness in ungodly ways. Ephesians 4:18 says, "They are darkened in their understanding, alienated from the life of God because of the ignorance that is in them, due to their hardness of heart."

I have seen many people turn away from God after a tragic experience. Such people not only have communication problems with God, but often have conflict with others. Their misguided outlook leads to broken marriages, separation from children, an inability to find employment, drug and alcohol abuse, and the list can go on and on.

My pain and disappointment caused me to have deep grief. Thankfully, I never lost sight of God. My emotional struggle caused me to try to maintain a close relationship with Christ. When I was in the darkness of despair, I held tightly to Jesus and trusted Him.

COMFORT THROUGH TROUBLESOME CIRCUMSTANCES

As a believer of Jesus Christ, I had hope in God's ability to change my outlook. Second Corinthians 5:17-18 says, "Therefore, if anyone is in Christ, he is a new creation. The old has passed away; behold, the new has come." When I am in a right relationship with God, He refreshes me through the Holy Spirit.

Because of His presence in me, and with the hope of a better tomorrow, I am motivated to trust God. Awareness of

Christ's promised return also encourages me to obey and follow Him.

As Isaiah 55:6-7 says, "Seek the LORD while he may be found; call upon him while he is near; let the wicked forsake his way, and the unrighteous man his thoughts; let him return to the LORD, that he may have compassion on him, and to our God, for he will abundantly pardon."

I am grateful how Jesus has transformed me. My emotional and spiritual life came close to the boundaries of despair. Yet my loss has also given me insights I otherwise would have missed.

Adversity causes me to trust God with what I hope for but have not received. Thankfully through the Holy Spirit, God comforts me with His peace when I am disappointed and confused by an unwanted outcome.

As Hebrews 10:23 reminds me, "Let us hold fast the confession of our hope without wavering, for he who promised is faithful." I am grateful God is my dependable anchor through painful circumstances. He is always faithful.

FOREWARNED OF AN IRREVERSIBLE DECLINE

Two days before Bonnie died, I called my workplace and asked coworkers to keep my daughter in prayer. The person I spoke with responded in a strange and unusual way which gave me needed insight.

He asked, "Have you ever watched someone die?"

I had cared for people before they died, but I had never watched an individual die. So, I answered my personnel director with a "No."

He mentioned how Bonnie's inability to swallow led him to believe she was near death. His description of the predictable process gave me insight to prepare myself for the undesired outcome.

My coworker went on to say that after her swallowing issue, the ability to breathe would become increasingly difficult. Sure enough, the next day my daughter struggled to take a deep breath.

His insight helped prepare me for Bonnie's death, but I never gave up on the hope that a miracle would happen. Nevertheless, I watched the natural process of physical death come upon her. I prepared myself for what happened due to an awareness of the likely responses that quickly occurred.

Moments before my only child died, her attending doctor told us that Bonnie had an exceptional heartbeat. The physician also mentioned there could be long pauses between one breath and the next.

A friend who heard the doctor's words kept a close watch on how Bonnie breathed. About five minutes later he noticed a change. So, I got the physician to come and check on Bonnie.

The doctor came immediately. He had a puzzled look on his face as he listened to Bonnie's heart with his stethoscope. Then the doctor opened her eyelids and used a light to check for a response. Sorrowfully and softly, he said, "I think she just passed."

Bonnie's death and quick departure reminds me how no one knows the day or hour when life on earth will end. God, on the other hand, possesses full knowledge of all my days. Nothing surprises God, and He promises to keep watch over those who love Him no matter what happens here on earth.

My trust in God has helped me to respond appropriately when unexpected and undesired circumstances happen. As the Holy Spirit reveals God's nearness to me, I follow Him as my LORD and Savior who loves me.

PURPOSE IN SORROW

When Bonnie died, I lost an irreplaceable part of my life. I am no longer able to enjoy her unique humor and insightful perspectives.

Memories of her expressions of genuine joy motivate me to appreciate every moment of my life. I am thankful how Bonnie influenced me by her outlook and regard for others.

As Bonnie grew up as a child I learned about her relationship with God. I asked my daughter how He showed Himself to her. The insights, sincerity, innocence, and honesty of her responses amazed me.

Those conversations provided me with a fresh and enjoyable outlook on life. After Bonnie permanently departed, I soon realized how much she had influenced me. Her death caused intense emotional pain in me.

I am grateful God did not keep me in my distressed condition. Psalm 107:14 reminds me, "He brought them out of darkness and the shadow of death, and burst their bonds apart." He turned my sorrow into joy.

As Bonnie's earthly father, I am grateful how my daughter lived for God. I hope my heavenly Father looks upon me in a similar manner.

Solomon summarized in Ecclesiastes 12:13 how the purpose of life is to fear God and obey His commandments. To be right with God does not happen naturally, by my good works, or by the number of friends I have.

God is the source of my strength when I am not able to change circumstances. Psalm 16:11 reminds me, "You make known to me the path of life; in your presence there is fullness of joy; at your right hand are pleasures forevermore." He gives me needed insight and assurance of His constant help in my life.

As Matthew 6:26 says, "Look at the birds of the air: they neither sow nor reap nor gather into barns, and yet your heavenly Father feeds them. Are you not of more value than they?" God loves me so much He allowed His only Son, Jesus Christ, to die on the cross for my sins. This shows the great value God places on me.

AN UNEXPECTED LIFT

Road trips have given me the opportunity to visit many different places. The southern shores of Michigan provided an unforgettable memory. Fine sandy soil surrounds the shore of Lake Michigan. Over the centuries, strong westerly winds have caused waves to crash against its shoreline to make large sand dunes.

My family watched hang gliders at a beach on Lake Michigan. The large kites gently lifted each of them out of the ankle-deep sand as they ran into the strong headwinds. Each person was lifted up and flew over the lake and the deep water below them.

We watched in silence as the gliders effortlessly sailed across the sky. After several minutes of flight, they returned and landed their hang glider on the beach.

While visiting friends in the Blue Ridge Mountains of Virginia, my daughter had a similar experience. As a child she had the opportunity to ride on a lightweight aircraft.

The Ultralight consisted of lightweight pipes, a small engine, two tiny seats with safety belts, and rubber tires.

The good friends we were with knew the person flying the Ultralight. When he landed, he offered to take one of us up for a ride. Bonnie jumped at the chance to fly with so much enthusiasm that Karen and I had to let her go up.

Karen and I watched in amazement as our daughter joined

the pilot and took off. The aircraft quickly became a tiny dot in the sky. Then we wondered to ourselves, "Why did we ever allow our only child do such a thing?"

Upon her return Bonnie immediately wanted to go up again. However, darkness began to fall, and she needed to get ready for bed.

As her parents we wanted our daughter to keep her feet on the ground. Yet for Bonnie, that aircraft ride became one of her most memorable childhood experiences.

Both the hang gliders and Ultralight aircraft offered no protection from an unexpected fall. The pilots on both needed to trust their small aircraft to fly and return them safely to the ground.

I also am reminded how strong forces of resistance cause me to turn to the Lord for a needed lift, to help me rise above my trials. My hardships motivate me to face difficult and stubborn obstacles with faith. As I do so, God helps me to overcome my doubts as the Holy Spirit upholds me.

God's inner strength empowers me to be secure when I experience hardship. I trust Him to get me through the obstacles that hinder my life. God is faithful and helps me rise above my problems. He gives me needed strength, hope, and endurance when I am in troublesome circumstances.

As 2 Corinthians 4:8-10 says, "We are afflicted in every way, but not crushed; perplexed, but not driven to despair; persecuted, but not forsaken; struck down, but not destroyed; always carrying in the body the death of Jesus, so that the life of Jesus may also be manifested in our bodies." Jesus carries me through my hardships.

Bonnie's best friend, Abby Mann Legge, wrote a poem about how she got through her sorrow and grief when Bonnie died. Her words express God's ability to lift her up when she was brokenhearted.

MIGHTY HAND

Human eyes like sifting sand
Scour the land for a mighty hand
And when they find that mighty hand
They expect peace throughout their land

But what they do not know
Is they will face many a foe
And for many highs, also lows
Those lows will bring unspeakable woes

But when it seems too much to bear
His hand reaches with utmost care
You see His presence everywhere
He calls us when we have nowhere

And when those eyes grow wet with tears
He stands by to calm all our fears
And when our muddied eyes thus clear
It's Him alone at front and rear

The hurt will soon be wiped away
When we see Him that perfect day
He who knows us in every way
Will lead us no matter what lay

Human eyes like sifting sand
Scour the land for a mighty hand
And since I found that mighty hand
I will walk on land or sand

Abby's poem reminds me of 2 Chronicles 16:9, "For the eyes of the LORD run to and fro throughout the whole earth, to give strong support to those whose heart is blameless towards him."

When I remember the shores of southern Lake Michigan, my memory thinks of soft dry sand dunes.

I need perseverance and determination to arrive at my destination when my situation is unstable.

Most people assume peace is experienced only in calm and uneventful times. Thankfully, God gives me the ability to rise above earthly obstacles even in the worst situations.

As 1 Peter 4:19 says, "Therefore let those who suffer according to God's will entrust their souls to a faithful Creator while doing good." God is always faithful. He lifted me up when I was at my lowest point. He will always be there for me.

WHEN THE END IS NEAR

Bonnie's last days on earth were far from peaceful. Nevertheless, God gave my entire family His peace. He gave us assurance of His love, mercy, and grace through our hardship. We did not let death overwhelm us. We never lost hope that Bonnie could be healed. Though Bonnie was not healed on earth, she was healed when God took her to heaven. Now she lives with Him.

Jesus reminded me in Matthew 22:31-32, "And as for the resurrection of the dead, have you not read what was said to you by God: 'I am the God of Abraham, and the God of Isaac, and the God of Jacob'? He is not God of the dead, but of the living."

Through faith in Christ's resurrection, He gave me a new life. I am born again. Since Jesus transformed my life, I look forward to when He will call me to my eternal home in heaven with Him.

First Peter 1:8-9 promises Christ's followers, "Though you have not seen him, you love him. Though you do not now see him, you believe in him and rejoice with joy that is inexpressible and filled with glory, obtaining the outcome of your faith, the salvation of your souls." Praise God, the best is yet to come!

When I came to faith in Christ, He forgave me of all my sins and set me apart as God's child. I am in no way perfect, yet His Son Jesus Christ promises eternal life to all who believe in Him.

I am grateful how the Holy Spirit empowers me to know God. The Spirit of God gives me peace in my trials and hope for the future. As Galatians 5:5 says, "For through the Spirit, by faith, we ourselves eagerly wait for the hope of righteousness." God plans to make all things beautiful in His time.

This God-given ability to be content in my troublesome circumstances reveals His love and goodness to me. He took the curse of death away and gave me His peace. I trust Him to help me in every hardship. He promises never to forsake me as I live for Him.

HELPFUL PROMISES AND ENCOURAGEMENT FOR THOSE WHO PURSUE GOD'S PEACE

"The LORD bless you and keep you; the LORD make his face to shine upon you and be gracious to you; the LORD lift up his countenance upon you and give you peace" Numbers 6:24-26.

"Turn away from evil and do good, seek peace and pursue it" Psalm 34:14.

"Let me hear what God the LORD will speak, for he will speak peace to his people, to his saints; but let them not turn to folly. Surely his salvation is near to those who fear him, that glory may dwell in our land" Psalm 85:8-9.

"Deceit is in the heart of those who devise evil, but those who plan peace have joy" Proverbs 12:20.

"You keep him in perfect peace whose mind is stayed on you, because he trusts in you. Trust in the LORD forever, for the LORD GOD is an everlasting rock" Isaiah 26:3-4.

"I have said these things to you, that in me you may have peace. In the world you will have tribulation. But take heart; I have overcome the world" John 16:33.

"Therefore, since we have been justified by faith, we have peace with God through our Lord Jesus Christ" Romans 5:1.

"Let your reasonableness be known to everyone. The Lord is at hand; do not be anxious about anything, but in everything by prayer and supplication with thanksgiving let your requests be made known to God. And the peace of God, which surpasses all understanding, will guard your hearts and your minds in Christ Jesus" Philippians 4:5-7.

"And let the peace of Christ rule in your hearts, to which indeed you were called in one body. And be thankful" Colossians 3:15.

"Now may the Lord of peace himself give you peace at all times in every way. The Lord be with you all" 2 Thessalonians 3:16.

ABOUT THE AUTHOR

Dr. James Szymanski plans to publish three more books in 2025 through Looking Up Press.

The Foundation of God's Word is a 365-day devotional. This book will include devotionals through every book of the Old Testament. This study engages a reader with God's proclamation to know He alone is LORD.

Empowered by God is a 365-day devotional through the New Testament. The message of salvation in Jesus Christ transforms believers as He empowers those who follow Him.

James also developed a children's book entitled, *Clare and Bear Battle Cancer*. This book looks at cancer from a child's perspective.

Currently, James is under observation for a "non-cancerous" brain tumor. He has received radiation and hopes the treatment will slow the growth of the tumor. James continues to find his comfort in God's promises found in the Holy Bible. Indeed, God is his ultimate Help in Hardship.

Made in the USA
Columbia, SC
22 April 2025

56955028R00124